SRI VISHNU SAHASRANAMA STHOTRAM

Sloka Book

JET Publisning House

INDIA   USA

TOWARDS EXCELLENCE

P
R
A
J
N
A

Title	SRI VISHNU SAHASRANAMA STHOTRAM
Subtitle	SLOKA BOOK
Copyright	Jeeyar Educational Trust
First Edition	2019
Contributor	His Holiness Chinna Jeeyar Swamiji

CONTACT US:

INDIA

JIVA
Sriramanagaram, Shamshabad,
R.R. Dist. Andhra Pradesh - 509 325
Phone: 95535 49971, 95535 499

UNITED STATES

JETUSA Inc.
Jeeyar Asram, 222, Dey Road,
CRANBURY, NJ 08512, USA
Phone:609-297-8797

Website: www.prajna4me.org   Email: prajna@jetusa.org

INTRODUCTION

To realize the Divine and use every bit of our knowledge and wealth in His service is a great boon in one's life. In the ecstatic state of Love towards God, a devotee feels the causeless compassion of the Divine and begins to pray Him and sing His glories in every possible way. Our great ancient Rishis, A:lwa:rs and A:cha:rya:s have experienced the Divine. They poured out their divine experiences in the form of sacred compositions delivered involuntarily, recorded by their followers. Bhagavad Githa and Sri Vishnu Sahasra Na:ma Stho:thram were the two gems hidden in the mighty ocean of Maha:bha:ratha. Lord Sri Krushna himself taught Bhagavad Githa to Arjuna. Whereas Sri Vishnu Sahasra Na:ma Stho:thram was revealed by Bhishma:charya to Pa:ndava:s when he was on the bed of arrows, after the Mahabharatha war.

Krushna took Pa:ndava:s to Bhishma and requested pitha:maha (grandsire) to teach the Pa:ndavas about the Ultimate Truth and Dharma. Bhishma was so weak physically and mentally being on the bed of arrows. Krushna promised pitha:maha Bhishma that He would restore his memory that was buried deep due to the pains in his body.

Pa:ndavas approached Bhishma to teach them the higher principles of life and wisdom, from all his great experiences. Bhishma, who is a great Man of Action and Sacrifice, mastered the whole Dharma Sa:sthra and practiced it strictly throughout his life. Even the Lord of Death feared to approach Bhishma without his permission. Dharmaraja asks him to tell them the greatest of the secrets that made him so great and that he thinks is the best that can liberate all beings from the cycle of birth and death, and lead them to reach the highest Happiness, Bliss, The Lord.

Then Bhishmacharya, having obtained boon from Lord Krushna to be able to speak in clear voice and memorize his past deeds, reveals the essence of all that he learnt from a number of sages who had the vision of Lord in different forms. Bhishma observed a number of austerities imposed by the sages, served them for long periods, satisfied them that he deserves to be taught the secret they have obtained after strenuous efforts, and finally obtained from them the secrets. Like a honeybee that collects the honey drops from all the flowers, Bhishmacharya collected all the manthras from different sages and composed Sri Vishnu Sahasra Na:ma Stho:thram, which he used to practice daily. When Dharmaraja asked him to reveal the greatest of secrets, Bhishma reveals this to Pa:ndavas on Magha Suddha Eka:dasi day in the presence of Lord Krushna, showing Him and telling them that He is Lord of all Lords and praying Him with all thousand names is all one can ever do to become more dear to Him which itself leads to salvation. Reciting it regularly or even listening to it is itself a great thing that empowers one with the strength to overcome all the difficulties and get on to the right path of salvation. As it was imparted from a

great acharya chosen by the Lord Himself, Sri Vishnu Sahasra Na:ma is considered the essence of Githa and all the Vedas.

In view of this, Acharya HH Sri Swamiji is conducting mass chanting of Sri Vishnu Sahasra Na:ma Stho:thram for the sake of world peace since 1994 to bless us all with the secret of the secrets and empower us with health, wealth and wisdom and to lead righteous and happy life. How fortunate we are if we are with our Acha:rya taking upade:sam from Him about the best of the secrets a man needs to know in his life!!

Jai Srimannarayana!

PRAJNA PLEDGE

Jai Srimannarayana!

O Mother Earth! I, being your best child and responsible citizen of this world, take this pledge!

I shall revere my parents, my family, my Gurus and treat everyone with love.

I shell serve my community, my country and those in need.

I pledge to protect the Nature by caring for animals, trees and the environment.

I will learn from the experiences of my ancestors and pass it on to future generations.

I, as student of Prajna, swear to abide by the universal commandments.

Worship your own and Respect all & Serve all beings as service to God.

Jai Srimannarayana!

Telugu	Hindi	English		Telugu	Hindi	English
అ	अ	a		ట	ट	ta
ఆ	आ	a:		ఠ	ठ	tta
ఇ	इ	i		ఠ	ट	**tta**
ఈ	ई	i:		డ	ड	**da**
ఉ	उ	u		ఢ	ढ	**dda**
ఊ	ऊ	u:		ఢ	ढ	**dha**
ఋ	ऋ	ru		ణ	ण	**na**
ౠ	ॠ	ru:		త	त	tha
ఌ	अलु	lu		థ	त्त	ththa
ౡ	अलू	lu:		• థ	स्थ	} ttha
ఎ		e		•• థ	ध	
ఏ	ए	e:		ద	द	da
ఐ	ऐ	ai		ధ	ह्द	dda
ఒ		o		ధ	ध्द	dha
ఓ	ओ	o:		న	न	na
ఔ	औ	au/ow		ప	प	pa
అం	अं	am		ఫ	फ	pha
అః	अः	aha		బ	ब	ba
క	क	ka		భ	भ	bha
ఖ	ख	kha		మ	म	ma
గ	ग	ga		య	य	ya
ఘ	घ	gha		ర	र	ra
ఙ	ङ	nga		ల	ल	la
చ	च	cha		వ	ब	va
ౘ	च	chcha		శ	श	sa
• ఛ	छ	} chha		ష	ष	sha
•• ఛ	छ			స	स	sa
జ	ज	ja		హ	ह	ha
ఝ	झ	jha		ళ	ळ	la
ఞ	ञ	ini		ఱ		rra
				క్ష	क्ष	ksha
				జ్ఞ		Jna

• This letter comes only in the middle of the word

• • This letter comes in the beginning/middle of the word

☞ Pronounciation of both these letters is almost similar

GURU PARAMPARA

srisaile:sa daya: pa:thram
dhi:bhakthya:di guna:rnavam|
yathi:ndra pravanam vande:
ramya ja:ma:tharam munim || 1

lakshmi: na:ttha sama:rambha:m
na:ttha ya:muna madhyama:m |
asmad a:cha:rya paryantha:m
vande: guru parampara:m || 2

yo: nithyam achyutha pada:mbuja yugma rukma
vya:mo:hathas thadithara:ni thruna:ya me:ne:|
asmadguro:r bhagavatho:sya dayaika sindho:ho
ra:ma:nujasya charanau saranam prapadye:|| 3

ma:tha: pitha: yuvathayas thanaya: vibhu:thihi
sarvam yade:va niyame:na madanvaya:na:m |
a:dyasya nah kulapathe:r vakula:bhira:mam
sri:math thadanghri yugalam pranama:mi mu:rdhna: || 4

bhu:tham saras cha mahada:hvaya bhattana:ttha
sri: bhakthi sa:ra kulase:khara yo:giva:ha:n |
bhaktha:nghri renu paraka:la yathi:ndra misra:n
srimath para:nkusa munim pranatho:smi nithyam || 5

Om bhagavanna:ra:yana:bhi matha:nuru:pa svaru:pa ru:pa
gunavibhava aisvaryasi:la:di anavadhika:thisaya
asankhye:ya kalya:na gunagana:m
padma vana:laya:m bhagavathi:m
sriyam de:vi:m nithya:na pa:yani:m
niravadya:m de:va de:va divya mahishi:m
akhila jaganma:tharam asanma:tharam asaranya saranya:m
ananya saranaha saranamaham prapadye: || 6

SRI: LAKSHMI ASHTO:THTHARA SATHA NA:MA STHO:THRAM

Dhya:nam

vande: padmakara:m prasanna vadana:m saubha:gyada:m bha:gyada:m
hastha:bhya:m abhayaprada:m maniganair na:na:vidhair bhu:shitha:m |
bhaktha:bhi:shta phalaprada:m   harihara brahma:dibhis se:vitha:m
pa:rsve: pankaja sankha padma nidhibhir yuktha:m sada: sakthibhihi ||

sarasija nayane: saro:ja hasthe:
dhavalathara:msuka gandha ma:lya so:bhe: |
bhagavathi harivallabhe: mano:jne:
thribhuvana bhu:thikari prasi:da mahyam ||

prakruthim vikruthim vidya:m   sarvabhu:tha hithaprada:m |
sraddha:m vibhu:thim surabhim   nama:mi parama:thmika:m || (1)

va:cham padma:laya:m padma:m   suchim sva:ha:m svadha:m sudha:m |
dhanya:m hiranmayi:m lakshmi:m   nithyapusta:m vibha:vari:m || (2)

adithim cha dithim di:ptha:m   vasudha:m vasudha:rini:m |
nama:mi kamala:m ka:ntha:m   kshama:m kshi:ro:da sambhava:m || (3)

anugraha para:m ruddhim   anagha:m hari vallabha:m |
aso:ka:m amrutha:m di:ptha:m   lo:kaso:ka vina:sini:m || (4)

nama:mi dharma nilaya:m   karuna:m lo:ka ma:tharam |
padma priya:m padma hastha:m   padma:kshi:m padma sundari:m || (5)

padmo:d bhava:m padma mukhi:m   padma na:bha priya:m rama:m |
padma ma:la:dhara:m de:vi:m   padmini:m padma gandhini:m || (6)

punya gandha:m suprasanna:m   prasa:da:bhi mukhi:m prabha:m |
nama:mi chandra vadana:m   chandra:m chandra saho:dari:m || (7)

chathur bhuja:m chandra ru:pa:m   indira:m indusi:thala:m |
a:hla:da janani:m pushtim   siva:m sivakari:m sathi:m || (8)

vimala:m visva janani:m thushtim da:ridrya na:sini:m |
pri:thi pushkarini:m sa:ntha:m sukla ma:lya:mbara:m sriyam || (9)

bh:askari:m bilvanilaya:m vara:ro:ha:m yasasvini:m |
vasundhara:m uda:ra:nga:m harini:m he:mama:lini:m || (10)

dhana dha:nyakari:m siddhim sthraina saumya:m subhaprada:m |
nrupave:sma gatha:nanda:m varalakshmi:m vasuprada:m || (11)

subha:m hiranyapra:ka:ra:m samudra thanaya:m jaya:m |
nama:mi mangala:m de:vi:m vishnu vakshas sthala sthitha:m || (12)

vishnupathni:m prasanna:kshi:m na:ra:yana sama:sritha:m |
da:ridrya dhvansini:m de:vi:m sarvo:padrava va:rini:m || (13)

navadurga:m maha:ka:li:m brahma vishnu siva:thmika:m |
thrika:la jna:na sampanna:m nama:mi bhuvane:svari:m || (14)

lakshmi:m kshi:ra samudra ra:ja thanaya:m sri:ranga dha:me:svari:m |
da:si:bhu:tha samastha de:va vanitha:m lo:kaika di:pa:nkura:m ||

sriman manda kata:ksha labdha vibhava brahme:ndra ganga:dhara:m |
thva:m thrailo:kya kutumbini:m sarasija:m vande: mukunda priya:m ||

ma:thar nama:mi kamale: kamala:yatha:kshi
   sri: vishnu hruth kamala va:sini viswa ma:thaha |
kshi:ro:daje: kamala ko:mala garbha gauri
   lakshmi! prasi:da sathatham namatha:m saranye: ||

   ithi sri: lakshmyashto:ththara sathana:ma stho:thram sampu:rnam |

PU:RVA PI:THIKA:-

sukla:mbaradharam vishnum sasivarnam chathur bhujam |
prasanna vadanam dhya:ye:th sarva vighno:pa sa:nthaye: || 1

yasya dvirada vakthra:dya:h pa:rishadya:h parassatham |
vighnam nighnanthi sathatham vishvakse:nam thama:sraye: || 2

vya:sam vasishtanaptha:ram sakthe:h pauthram akalmasham |
para:sara:thmajam vande: sukatha:tham thapo:nidhim || 3

vya:sa:ya vishnuru:pa:ya vya:saru:pa:ya vishnave: |
namo: vai bramhanidhaye: va:sishta:ya namo: namaha || 4

avika:ra:ya suddha:ya nithya:ya parama:thmane: |
sadaika ru:pa ru:pa:ya vishnave: sarvajishnave: || 5

yasya smarana ma:thre:na janma samsa:ra bandhana:th |
vimuchyathe: namas thasmai vishnave: prabha vishnave: || 6

o:m namo: vishnave: prabha vishnave: ||

sri: vaisampa:yana uva:cha –
sruthva: dharma:n aseshe:na pa:vana:ni cha sarvasaha |
yudhishtiras sa:nthanavam punare:va:bhya bha:shatha || 7

yudhishtira uva:cha –
kime:kam daivatham lo:ke: kim va:pye:kam para:yanam |
sthuvanthah kam kam archanthah pra:pnuyur ma:nava:ssubham || 8

ko: dharmas sarva dharma:na:m bhavathah paramo: mathaha |
kim japan muchyathe: janthur janma samsa:ra bandhana:th || 9

sri: bhi:shma uva:cha –
jagath prabhum de:va de:vam anantham purusho:ththamam |
sthuvan na:ma sahasre:na purushas sathatho:ththithaha || 10

thame:va cha:rchayan nithyam bhakthya: purusham avyayam |
dhya:yan sthuvan namasyamscha yajama:nas thame:va cha || 11

ana:di nidhanam vishnum sarvalo:ka mahe:svaram |
lo:ka:dhyaksham sthuvan nithyam sarva duhkha:thigo: bhave:th || 12

brahma**n**yam sarva dharmajnam lo:ka:na:m ki:rthi vardhanam |
lo:kana:**th**am mahadbhu:tham sarvabhu:tha bhavo:d bhavam || 13

e:sha me: sarva dharma:**n**a:m dharmo:dhikathamo: mathaha |
yadbhakthya: pu**n**dari:ka:ksham sthavair arche:n narassada: || 14

paramam yo: mahaththe:jaha paramam yo: mahaththapaha |
paramam yo: mahadbramha paramam yah para:ya**n**am || 15

pavithra:**n**a:m pavithram yo: mangala:**n**a:m cha mangalam |
daivatham de:vatha:na:m cha bhu:tha:na:m yo:vyayah pitha: || 16

yatha ssarva:**n**i bhu:tha:ni bhavanthya:di yuga:game: |
yasmim**s**cha pra**l**ayam ya:nthi punare:va yugakshaye: || 17

thasya lo:kapradha:nasya jaganna:dhasya bhu:pathe: |
vish**no**:r na:ma sahasram me: sru**n**u pa:pa bhaya:paham || 18

ya:ni na:ma:ni gau**n**a:ni vikhya:tha:ni maha:thmanaha |
rushibhih parigi:tha:ni tha:ni vakshya:mi bhu:thaye: || 19

vish**no**:r na:ma sahasrasya ve:davya:so: maha:n rushihi |
chando:nushtup tha**th**a: de:vo: bhagava:n de:vaki:suthaha || 20

amrutha:m **su**:dbhavo: bi:jam **s**akthir de:vaki nandanaha |
thrisa:ma: hrudayam thasya **s**a:nthyar**the**: viniyujyathe: || 21

vish**n**um jish**n**um maha:vish**n**um prabha vish**n**um mahe:**s**varam |
ane:karu:pa daithya:ntham nama:mi purusho:ththamam || 22

asya **s**ri:vish**no**:r divya sahasra na:ma stho:thra maha:manthrasya,
sri: ve:davya:so: bhagava:n rushihi, anushtup **ch**andaha,
sri: maha: vish**n**uh parama:thma: **s**ri:manna:ra:ya**n**o: de:vatha:,
amrutha:m **su**:dbhavo: bha:nurithi bi:jam, de:vaki: nandanas srashte:thi **s**akthihi,
udbhavaha ksho:bha**n**o: de:va ithi paramo: manthraha,
sankha bhrunnandaki: chakri:thi ki:lakam, **s**a:rngadhanva: gada:dhara ithyasthram,
ra**th**a:ngapa:ni raksho:bhya ithi ne:thram, thrisa:ma:
sa:magas sa:me:thi kavacham, a:nandam para brahme:thi yo:nihi,
ruthussudarsanah ka:la ithi digbandhaha, **s**ri: viswaru:pa ithi dhya:nam,
sri: maha: vish**n**u kainkarya ru:pe: **s**ri: sahasra na:ma jape: viniyo:gaha ||

Dhya:nam

kshi:ro:danvath prade:se: suchimani vilasath saikathe: maukthika:na:m
ma:la: kluptha:sanasthaha sphatika mani nibhair maukthikair manditha:ngaha |
subhrair abhrair adabhrair upari virachithair muktha pi:yu:sha varshaihi
a:nandi: nah puni:ya:d arinalina gada: sankha pa:nir mukundaha || 24

bhu:hpa:dau yasya na:bhir viyad asuranilas chandra su:ryau cha ne:thre:
karna: va:sa:ssiro:dyaur mukhamapi dahano: yasya va:sthe:yam abdhihi |
anthastham yasya viswam sura nara khaga go: bho:gi gandharva daithyaihi
chithram ram ramyathe: tham thribhuvana vapusham vishnumi:sam nama:mi || 25

sa:ntha:ka:ram bhujaga sayanam padmana:bham sure:sam
viswa:ka:ram gagana sadrusam me:ghavarnam subha:ngam |
lakshmi:ka:ntham kamala nayanam yo:gi hruddhya:na gamyam
vande: vishnum bhava bhaya haram sarva lo:kaika na:tham || 26

me:ghasya:mam pi:tha kause:ya va:sam
sri:vathsa:nkam kausthubho:d bha:sitha:ngam |
punyo:pe:tham pundari:ka:ya tha:ksham
vishnum vande: sarva lo:kaika na:tham || 27

sa sankha chakram sa kiri:ta kundalam
sa pi:tha vasthram sarasi:ru he:kshanam |
saha:ra vakshasthala so:bhi kausthubham
nama:mi vishnum sirasa: chathur bhujam || 28

Harihi O:m!

visvam vishnur vashatka:ro: bhu:tha bhavya bhavath prabhuhu |
bhu:thakrud bhu:thabhrud bha:vo: bhu:tha:thma: bhu:tha bha:vanaha || 1

pu:tha:thma parama:thma: cha muktha:na:m parama:gathihi |
avyayah purushas sa:kshi: kshe:thrajno: akshara e:va cha || 2

yo:go: yo:gavida:m ne:tha: pradha:na purushe:svaraha |
na:rasimhavapus sri:ma:n ke:savah purusho:ththmaha || 3

sarvas sarvas sivas stha:nuhu bhu:tha:dir nidhiravyayaha |
sambhavo: bha:vano: bhartha: prabhavah prabhur i:svaraha || 4

svayambhu:s sambhur a:dithyah pushkara:ksho: maha:svanaha |
ana:di nidhano: dha:tha: vidha:tha: dha:thur uththamaha || 5

aprame:yo: hrushi:ke:sah padmana:bho: amaraprabhuhu |
visvakarma: manus thvashta: sthavishtas sthaviro: dhruvaha || 6

agra:hyas sa:svathah krushno: lo:hitha:kshah prathardanaha |
prabhu:thas thrikakubdha:ma pavithram mangalam param || 7

I:sa:nah pra:nadah pra:no: jye:shtas sre:shtah praja:pathihi |
hiranyagarbho: bhu:garbho: ma:dhavo: madhusu:danaha || 8

I:svaro: vikrami: dhanvi: me:dha: vi: vikramah kramaha |
anuththamo: dura:dharshaha kruthajnah kruthir a:thmava:n || 9

sure:sas saranam sarma visvare:tha:h praja: bhavaha |
ahas samvathsaro: vya:laha prathyayas sarva darsanaha || 10

ajas sarve: svaras siddhas siddhis sarva:dir achyuthaha |
vrusha:kapir ame:ya:thma: sarvayo:ga vinissruthaha || 11

vasur vasumana:s sathyas sama:thma: sammithas samaha |
amo:ghah pundari:ka:ksho: vrushakarma: vrusha:kruthihi || 12

rudro: bahusira: babhruhu visvayo:nis suchissrava:ha |
amruthas sa:svathas stha:nuhu vara:ro:ho: maha:thapa:ha || 13

sarvagas sarvavid bha:nuhu vishvakse:no: jana:rdanaha |
ve:do: ve:david avyango: ve:da:ngo: ve:davith kavihi ||

14

lo:ka:dhyakshas sura:dhyaksho: dharma:dhyakshah krutha:kruthaha |
chathura:thma: chathurvyu:has chathur damshtras chathurbhujaha ||

15

bhra:jishnur bho:janam bho:ktha: sahishnur jagada:dijaha |
anagho: vijayo: je:tha: visvayo:nih punarvasuhu ||

16

upe:ndro: va:manah pra:msuhu amo:ghas suchir u:rjithaha |
athi:ndras sangrahas sargo: dhrutha:thma: niyamo: yamaha ||

17

ve:dyo: vaidyas sada:yo:gi: vi:raha: ma:dhavo: madhuhu |
athi:ndriyo: maha:ma:yo: maho:thsa:ho: maha:balaha ||

18

maha:buddhir maha:vi:ryo: maha:sakthir maha:dyuthihi |
anirde:syavapus sri:ma:n ame:ya:thma: maha:dridhruth ||

19

mahe:shva:so: mahi:bhartha: sri:niva:sas satha:m gathihi |
aniruddhas sura:nando: go:vindo: go:vida:m pathihi ||

20

mari:chir damano: hamsaha suparno: bhujago:ththamaha |
hiranyana:bhas suthapa:h padmana:bhah praja:pathihi ||

21

amruthyus sarvadruk simhaha sandha:tha: sandhima:n sthiraha |
ajo: durmarshanas sa:stha: visrutha:thma: sura:riha: ||

22

gurur guruthamo: dha:ma sathyas sathya para:kramaha |
nimisho: animishas sragvi: va:chaspathir uda:radhi:hi ||

23

agrani:r gramani:s sri:ma:n nya:yo: ne:tha: sami:ranaha |
sahasra mu:rdha: visva:thma: sahasra:kshas sahasra pa:th ||

24

a:varthano: nivruththa:thma: samvruthas sampra mardanaha |
ahas samvarthako: vanhir anilo: dharani:dharaha ||

25

suprasa:dah prasanna:thma: visvasrud visvabhug vibhuhu |
sathkartha: sathkruthas sa:dhuhu janhur na:ra:yano: naraha ||

26

asankhye:yo: aprame:ya:thma: visishtas sishtakruch chuchihi |
siddha:rthas siddha sankalpaha siddhidas siddhi sa:dhanaha ||

27

vrusha:hi: vrishabho: vishnuhu vrusha parva: vrusho:daraha |
vardhano: vardha ma:nascha vivikthas sruthi sa:garaha || 28

subhujo: durdharo: va:gmi: mahe:ndro: vasudo: vasuhu |
naikaru:po: bruhad ru:paha sipivishtah praka:sanaha || 29

o:jas the:jo: dyuthi dharah praka:sa:thma pratha:panaha |
ruddhas spashta:ksharo: manthraha chandra:msur bha:skara dyuthihi || 30
amrutha:m su:dhbhavo: bha:nuhu sasibindus sure:svaraha |
aushadham jagathas se:thuhu sathya dharma para:kramaha || 31

bhu:tha bhavya bhavan na:tthaha pavanah pa:vano: analaha |
ka:maha: ka:makruth ka:nthaha ka:mah ka:mapradah prabhuhu || 32

yuga:dikrud yuga:vartho: naikama:yo: maha:sanaha |
adrusyo: vyaktharu:pascha sahasrajid ananthajith || 33

ishto: avisishtas sishte:shtah sikhandi: nahusho: vrushaha |
kro:dhaha: kro:dha kruth kartha: visvaba:hur mahi:dharaha || 34

achyuthah prathithah pra:naha pra:nado: va:sava:nujaha |
apa:mnidhir adhishta:nam apramaththah prathishtithaha || 35

skandas skandadharo: dhuryo: varado: va:yu va:hanaha |
va:sude:vo bruhad bha:nuhu a:dide:vah purandaraha || 36

aso:kas tha:ranas tha:raha su:ras saurir jane:svaraha |
anuku:las satha:varthah padmi: padma nibhe:kshanaha || 37

padma na:bho: aravinda:kshah padma garbhas sari:rabhruth |
mahardhir ruddho: vruddha:thma: maha:ksho: garuda dhvajaha || 38

athulas sarabho: bhi:maha samayajno: havir harihi |
sarva lakshana lakshanyo: lakshmi:va:n samithinjayaha || 39

viksharo: ro:hitho: ma:rgo: he:thur da:mo:daras sahaha |
mahi:dharo: maha:bha:go: ve:gava:n amitha:sanaha || 40

udbhavah ksho:bhano: de:vaha sri:garbhah parame:svaraha |
karanam ka:ranam kartha: vikartha: gahano: guhaha || 41

vyavasa:yo: vyavastha:naha samstha:nas stha:nado: dhruvaha |
parardhih paramas spashtaha thushtah pushtas subhe:kshanaha ||

42

ra:mo: vira:mo: virajo: ma:rgo: ne:yo: nayo: anayaha |
vi:ras sakthi matha:m sre:shto: dharmo: dharmavid uththamaha ||

43

vaikuntah purushah pra:naha pra:nadah pranavah pruthuhu |
hiranya garbhas sathrughno: vya:ptho: va:yur adho:kshajaha ||

44

ruthus sudarsanah ka:laha parame:shti: parigrahaha |
ugras samvathsaro: daksho: visra:mo: visva dakshinaha ||

45

vistha:ras stha:vara stha:nuh prama:nam bi:jam avyayam |
artho: :nartho: maha:ko:so: maha:bho:go: maha:dhanaha ||

46

anirvinnas sthahvishto: bhu:hu dharma yu:po: maha: makhaha |
nakshathra ne:mir nakshathri: kshamaha ksha:mas sami:hanaha ||

47

yajna ijyo: mahe:jyascha krathus sathram satha:m gathihi |
sarvadarsi: nivruththa:thma: sarvajno: jna:nam uththamam ||

48

suvrathas sumukhas su:kshmaha sugho:shas sukhadas suhruth |
mano:haro: jithakro:dho: vi:raba:hur vida:ranaha ||

49

sva:panas svavaso: vya:pi: naika:thma: naika karmakruth |
vathsaro: vathsalo: vathsi: rathna garbho: dhane:svaraha ||

50

dharmagub dharmakrud dharmi: sad-aksharam-asath-ksharam |
avijna:tha: sahasra:msuhu vidha:tha: krutha lakshanaha ||

51

gabhasthi ne:mis sathvasthaha simho: bhu:tha mahe:svaraha |
a:dide:vo: maha:de:vo: de:ve:so: de:vabhrud guruhu ||

52

uththaro: go:pathir go:ptha: jna:na gamyah pura:thanaha |
sari:ra bhu:tha bhrud bho:ktha: kapi:ndro: bhu:ri dakshinaha ||

53

so:mapo: amruthapas so:maha purujith puru saththamaha |
vinayo: jayas sathya sandho: da:sa:rhas sa:thvatha:m pathihi ||

54

ji:vo: vinayitha: sa:kshi: mukundo: :mitha vikramaha |
ambho:nidhir anantha:thma: maho:dadhi sayo::nthakaha ||

55

ajo: maha:rhas sva:bha:vyo: jitha:mithrah pramo:danaha |
a:nando: nandano: nandaha sathya dharma: thrivikramaha ||

56

maharshih kapila:cha:ryaha kruthajno: me:dini:pathihi |
thripadas thridasa:dhyakshaha maha:srungah krutha:ntha kruth ||

57

maha:vara:ho: go:vindaha sushe:nah kanaka:ngadi: |
guhyo: gabhi:ro: gahano: gupthas chakra gada: dharaha ||

58

ve:dha:s sva:ngo::jithah krushno: drudhas sankarshano::chyuthaha |
varuno: va:runo: vrukshah pushkara:ksho: maha: mana:ha ||

59

bhagava:n bhagaha: nandi: vanama:li: hala:yudhaha |
a:dithyo: jyothir a:dithyaha sahishnur gathi saththamaha ||

60

sudhanva: khanda parasuhu da:runo: dravina pradaha |
divispruk sarvadrug vya:so: va:chaspathir ayo:nijaha ||

61

thrisa:ma: sa:magas sa:ma nirva:nam bhe:shajam bhishak |
sannya:sakruch chamas sa:ntho: nishta: sa:nthih para:yanaha ||

62

subha:ngas sa:nthidas srashta: kumudah kuvale:sayaha |
go:hitho: go:pathir go:ptha: vrushabha:ksho: vrusha priyaha ||

63

anivarthi: nivruththa:thma: sankshe:ptha: kshe:makruch chivaha |
sri:vathsa vaksha:s sri:va:saha sri:pathis sri:matha:m varaha ||

64

sri:das sri:sas sri:niva:saha sri:nidhis sri:vibha: vanaha |
sri:dharas sri:karas sre:yaha sri:ma:n lo:ka thraya:srayaha ||

65

svakshas svangas satha:nando: nandir jyothir gane:svaraha |
vijitha:thma: vidhe:ya:thma: sathki:rthis chinna samsayaha ||

66

udi:rnas sarvathas chakshuhu ani:sas sa:svatha sthiraha |
bhu:sayo: bhu:shano: bhu:thihi viso:kas so:ka na:sanaha ||

67

archishma:n archithah kumbho: visuddha:thma: viso:dhanaha |
aniruddho::prathi rathaha pradyumno::mitha vikramaha ||

68

ka:lane:miniha: saurihi su:ras su:rajane:svaraha |
thrilo:ka:thma: thrilo:ke:saha ke:savah ke:siha: harihi ||

69

ka:ma de:vah ka:ma pa:lah ka:mi: ka:nthah krutha:gamaha |
anirde:syavapur vishnuhu vi:ro::nantho: dhananjayaha || 70

bramhanyo: bramhakrud bramha: bramha bramha vivardhanaha |
bramhavid bra:mhano: bramhi: bramhajno: bra:mhana priyaha || 71

maha:kramo: maha:karma: maha:the:ja: maho:ragaha |
maha:krathur maha:yajva: maha:yajno: maha:havihi || 72

sthavyas sthavapriyas stho:thram sthuthas stho:tha: ranapriyaha |
pu:rnah pu:rayitha: punyah punyaki:rthir ana:mayaha || 73

mano:javas thi:rthakaro: vasure:tha: vasu pradaha |
vasuprado: va:sude:vo: vasur vasumana: havihi || 74

sadgathis sathkruthis saththa: sadbhu:this sathpara:yanaha |
su:rase:no: yadusre:shtaha sanniva:sas suya:munaha || 75

bhu:tha:va:so: va:sudevaha sarva:sunilayo: :nalaha |
darpaha: darpado: druptho: durdharo::tha::para:jithaha || 76

visva mu:rthir maha: mu:rthihi di:ptha mu:rthir amu:rthima:n |
ane:ka mu:rthir avyakthaha satha mu:rthis satha:nanaha || 77

e:ko: naikas sa vah kah kim yath thath padam anuththamam |
lo:ka bandhur lo:kana:tho: ma:dhavo: bhaktha vathsalaha || 78

suvarnavarno: he:ma:ngo: vara:ngas chandana:ngadi: |
vi:raha: vishamas su:nyo: ghrutha:si:r achalas chalaha || 79

ama:ni: ma:nado: ma:nyo: lo:ka sva:mi: thrilo:ka dhruth |
sume:dha: me:dhajo: dhanyaha sathya me:dha: dhara:dharaha || 80

the:jo:vrusho: dyuthidharaha sarva-sasthra-bhrutha:m-varaha |
pragraho: nigraho: vyagro: naikasrungo: gada:grajaha || 81

chathur mu:rthis chathur ba:huhu chathur vyu:has chathur gathihi |
chathur a:thma: chathur bha:vaha chathur ve:da vide:kapa:th || 82

sama:vartho: nivruththa:thma: durjayo: durathi-kramaha |
durlabho: durgamo: durgo: dura:va:so: dura:riha: || 83

subha:ngo: lo:kasa:rangaha suthanthus thanthu-vardhanaha |
indra karma: maha: karma: krutha karma: krutha:gamaha || 84

udbhavas sundaras sundo: rathna na:bhas sulo:chanaha |
arko: va:jasanis srungi: jayanthas sarva vijjayi: || 85

suvarna bindur aksho:bhyaha sarva-va:gi:sva re:svaraha |
maha:hrado: maha:gartho: maha:bhu:tho: maha:nidhihi || 86

kumudah kundarah kundah parjanyah pa:vano::nilaha |
amrutha:so::mrutha vapuhu sarvajnas sarvatho: mukhaha || 87

sulabhas suvrathas siddhaha sathru jicchathru tha:panaha |
nyagro:dho: dumbaro: : svatthaha cha:nu:ra:ndhra nishu:danaha || 88

sahasra:rchis sapthajihvaha sapthaidha:s saptha-va:hanaha |
amu:rthir anagho::chinthyo: bhayakruth bhaya na:sanaha || 89

anur bruhath krusas sthu:lo: gunabhrun nirguno: maha:n |
adhruthas svadhruthas sva:sthyaha pra:gvamso: vamsa-vardhanaha || 90

bha:ra bhruth kathitho: yo:gi: yo:gi:sas sarva ka:madaha |
a:sramas sramanah ksha:maha suparno: va:yu va:hanaha || 91

dhanur dharo: dhanur ve:do: dando: damayitha::damaha |
apara:jithas sarvasaho: niyantha: niyamo: yamaha || 92

sathvava:n sa:thvikas sathyaha sathya dharma para:yanaha |
abhipra:yah priya:rho:rhaha priyakruth pri:thi vardhanaha || 93

viha:yasagathir jyo:thihi suruchir huthabhug vibhuhu |
ravir vilo:chanas su:ryaha savitha: ravilo:chanaha || 94

anantha hutha bhug bho:ktha: sukhado: naikado: :grajaha |
anirvinnas sada:marshi: lo:ka:dhishta:nam adbhuthaha || 95

sana:th sana:thana thamaha kapilah kapir avyayaha |
svasthidas svasthi kruth svasthi svasthi bhuk svasthi dakshinaha || 96

araudrah kundali: chakri: vikramyu:rjitha sa:sanaha |
sabda:thigas sabda sahaha sisiras sarvari:karaha || 97

akru:rah pe:salo: daksho: dakshinaha kshamina:m varaha |
vidvaththamo: vi:thabhayaha punyas sravana ki:rthanaha || 98

uththa:rano: dushkruthiha: punyo: dussvapna na:sanaha |
vi:raha: rakshanas santho: ji:vanah paryavasthithaha || 99

anantharu:po::nanthasri:hi jithamanyur bhaya:pahaha |
chathurasro: gabhi:ra:thma: vidiso: vya:diso: disaha || 100

ana:dir bhu:rbhuvo: lakshmi:hi suvi:ro: ruchira:ngadaha |
janano: jana janma:dihi bhi:mo: bhi:ma para:kramaha || 101

a:dha:ranilayo: dha:tha: pushpa ha:sah praja:garaha |
u:rdhvagas sathpatha:cha:rah pra:nadah pranavah panaha || 102

prama:nam pra:nanilayaha pra:nadhruth pra:naji:vanaha |
thathvam thathvavid e:ka:thma: janma mruthyu jara:thigaha || 103

bhu:rbhuva svastharus tha:raha savitha: prapitha:mahaha |
yajno: yajnapathir yajva: yajna:ngo: yajna va:hanaha || 104

yajna bhruth yajna kruth yajni: yajna bhuk yajna sa:dhanaha |
yajna:ntha krud yajna guhyam annam anna:da e:va cha || 105
a:thma yo:nis svayam ja:tho: vaikha:nas sa:ma ga:yanaha |
de:vaki: nandanas srashta: kshithi:sah pa:pana:sanaha || 106

sankha bhrunnandaki: chakri: sa:rnga dhanva: gada:dharaha |
ratha:ngapa:nir aksho:bhyaha sarva praharana:yudhaha || (2 times)   107

sri: sarvapraharana:yudha o:m nama ithi |

vanama:li: gadi: sa:rngi: sankhi: chakri: cha nandaki: |
sri:ma:n na:ra:yano: vishnuhu va:sude:vo::bhi rakshathu || (2 times)   108

UTHTHARA PI:THIKA:

ithi:dam ki:rthani:yasya ke:savasya maha:thmanaha |
na:mna:m sahasram divya:na:m ase:she:na praki:rthitham ||
1

ya idam srunuya:n nithyam yascha:pi pariki:rthaye:th |
na:subham pra:pnuya:th kinchith so: muthre:ha cha ma:navaha ||
2

ve:da:nthago: bra:hmanas sya:th kshathriyo: vijayi: bhave:th |
vaisyo: dhana samrudhassya:th su:dras sukham-ava:pnuya:th ||
3

dharma:rthi: pra:pnuya:d dharmam artha:rthi: cha:rtham a:pnuya:th |
ka:ma:n ava:pnuya:th ka:mi: praja:rthi: cha:pnuya:th praja:ha ||
4

bhakthima:n yas sado:ttha:ya suchis thadgatha-ma:nasaha |
sahasram va:sude:vasya na:mna:m e:thath praki:rthaye:th ||
5

yasah pra:pno:thi vipulam ya:thi pra:dha:nyam e:vacha |
achala:m sriyam a:pno:thi sre:yah pra:pno: thyanuththamam ||
6

na bhayam kvachid a:pno:thi vi:ryam thejascha vindathi |
bhavathyaro:go: dyuthima:n balaru:pa-guna:nvithaha ||
7

ro:ga:rtho: muchyathe: ro:ga:th baddho: muchye:tha bandhana:th |
bhaya:n muchye:tha bhi:thasthu muchye:da:panna a:padaha ||
8

durga:nyathitharathya:su purushah purusho:ththamam |
sthuvan na:masahasre:na nithyam Bhakthi samanvithaha ||
9

va:sude:va:srayo: marthyo: va:sude:va para:yanaha |
sarvapa:pa visuddha:thma: ya:thi brahma sana:thanam ||
10

na va:sude:va baktha:na:m asubham vidyathe: kvachith |
janma mruthyu jara: vya:dhi bhayam naivo:paja:yathe: ||
11

imam sthavam adhi:ya:naha sraddha: bhakthi samanvithaha |
yujye:tha:thma sukha ksha:nthi sri: dhruthi smruthi ki:rthibhihi ||
12

na kro:dho: na cha ma:thsaryam na lo:bho: na: asubha:mathihi |
bhavanthi krutha punya:na:m bhaktha:na:m purusho:ththame: ||
13

dyaus sachandra:rka nakshathram kham diso: bhu:r maho:dadhihi |
va:sude:vasya vi:rye:na vidhrutha:ni maha:thmanaha ||
14

sa sura:sura gandharvam sa yaksho:raga ra:kshasam |
jagadvase: varthathe:dam krushnasya sa chara:charam ||
15

indriya:ni mano: buddhihi sathvam the:jo: balam dhruthihi |

va:sude:va:thma ka:nya:huhu . kshe:thram kshe:thrajna e:va cha || 16

sarva:gama:na:m a:cha:rah prathamam parikalpithaha |
a:cha:ra prabhavo: dharmo: dharmasya prabhur achyuthaha || 17

rushayah pitharo: de:va:ha maha:bhu:tha:ni dha:thavaha |
jangama:jangamam che:dam jagan na:ra:yano:dbhavam || 18

yo:go: jna:nam thatha: sa:nkhyam vidya:s silpa:di karma cha |
ve:da:s sa:sthra:ni vijna:nam e:thath sarvam jana:rdana:th || 19

e:ko: vishnur mahad bhu:tham pruthak bhu:tha:nyane:kasaha |
thri:n lo:ka:n vya:pya bhu:tha:thma: bhunkthe: visvabhug avyayaha || 20

imam sthavam bhagavatho: vishno:r vya:se:na ki:rthitham |
pate:dya ichche:th purushaha sre:yah pra:pthum sukha:ni cha || 21

visve:svaram ajam de:vam jagathah prabhum avyayam |
bhajanthi ye: pushkara:ksham na the: ya:nthi para:bhavam || 22

na the: ya:nthi para:bhavam o:m nama ithi

Arjuna uva:cha -

padmapathra! visa:la:ksha! padmana:bha! suro:ththama! |
baktha:na:m anuraktha:na:m thra:tha: bhava jana:rdana! || 23

Sri Bhagava:n uva:cha -

yo: ma:m na:masahasre:na stho:thum ichchathi pa:ndava! |
so:ham e:ke:na slo:ke:na sthutha e:va na samsayaha || 24

sthutha e:va na samsaya o:m nama ithi

Vya:sa uva:cha-

va:sana:d va:su:de:vasya va:sitham the: jagaththrayam |
sarva bhu:tha niva:so:si va:sude:va! namo:sthu the: || 25

Sri va:sude:va! namo:sthu tha o:m nama ithi

Pa:rvathyuva:cha-

ke:no:pa:ye:na laghuna: vishno:r na:ma sahasrakam |
patyathe: pandithair nithyam sro:thum ichcha:myaham prabho:! || 26

I:svara uva:cha-

sri:ra:ma ra:ma ra:me:thi rame:! ra:me mano:rame:! |
sahasra na:ma thath thulyam ra:ma na:ma vara:nane:! || 2 times 27

Sri: ra:mana:ma vara:nana o:m nama ithi

Brahmo:va:cha-

namo:s thvanantha:ya sahasra mu:rthaye:
sahasra pa:da:kshi siro:ru ba:have: |
sahasra na:mne: purusha:ya sa:svathe:
sahasrako:ti yuga dha:rine: namaha || 28

sri: sahasrako:ti yugadha:rina o:m nama ithi

Sanjaya uva:cha-

yathra yo:ge:svarah krushno: yathra pa:rtho: dhanur dharaha |
thathra sri:r vijayo: bhu:thihi   dhruva: ni:thir mathir mama || 29

Sri: Bhagava:n uva:cha-

ananya:s chinthayantho: ma:m   ye: jana:h paryupa:sathe: |
the:sha:m nithya:bhi yuktha:na:m   yo:gakshe:mam vaha:myaham || 30

parithra:na:ya sa:dhu:na:m   vina:sa:ya cha dushkrutha:m |
dharma samsttha:pana:rtha:ya   sambhava:mi yuge: yuge: || 31

a:rtha: vishanna:s sithila:scha bhi:tha:ha
gho:re:shu cha: vya:dhishu varthama:na:ha |
sanki:rthya na:ra:yana sabdama:thram
vimuktha duhkha:ha sukhino: bhavanthi || 32

yadakshara padabhrashtam   ma:thra:hi:nam thu yad bhave:th |
thath sarvam kshamyatha:m de:va!   na:ra:yana! namo:sthu the: || 33

ka:ye:na va:cha: manase:ndriyairva:
budhya:thmana:va: prakruthe:s svabha:va:th
karo:mi yadyath sakalam parasmai
na:ra:yana:ye:thi samarpaya:mi ||

sri:manna:ra:yana:ye:thi samarpaya:mi

sarvam sri: krushna:rpanamasthu

O:m asmath gurubhyo: namaha

SRI VISHNU SAHASRANA:MA
STHO:THRAM

visvam vishnur vashatka:ro: bhu:tha bhavya bhavath prabhuhu |
bhu:thakrud bhu:thabhrud bha:vo: bhu:tha:thma: bhu:tha bha:vanaha || 1

MEANINGS

Visvam	=	Full in all respects
Vishnuhu	=	One who pervades
Vashatka:raha	=	One who controls and directs (not merely pervades)
Bhu:tha bhavya bhavath prabhuhu	=	The Master of all things in the past, future and present
Bhu:thakruth	=	The creator of all beings
Bhu:thabhruth	=	The creator of all beings. He creates all things without depending on anything else
Bha:vah	=	He who exists
Bhu:tha:thma:	=	The soul of all beings
Bhu:tha bha:vanaha	=	He who nourishes all beings

pu:tha:thma parama:thma: cha muktha:na:m parama:gathihi |
avyayah purushas sa:kshi: kshe:thrajno: akshara e:va cha || 2

MEANINGS

Pu:tha:thma:	=	The Pure Self
Parama:thma:	=	The Supreme Soul
Muktha:na:m parama:gathihi	=	He who is thus the Supreme goal for all the Released Souls (Mukthas).
Avyayaha	=	He by whom Muktha is not sent away
Purushaha	=	The generous Giver
Sa:kshi:	=	He who sees them all directly
Kshe:thrajnah	=	The knower of the field for action
Aksharaha	=	He who never wanes

yo:go: yo:gavida:m ne:tha: pradha:na purushe:svaraha |
na:rasimhavapus sri:ma:n ke:savah purusho:ththmaha || 3

MEANINGS

Yo:gaha	=	He who is the Means
Yo:ga-Vida:m Ne:tha	=	He who leads those who practice yo:ga
Pradha:na purusha i:svaraha	=	The Lord of Primordial Matter and Purusha:s (i.e.Ji:va:s)
Na:rasimha-Vapuhu	=	He who is possessed of a body of man and lion combined
Sri:ma:n	=	He of a lovely form
Ke:savaha	=	He who has lovely locks of hair
Purusho:ththamaha	=	The Supreme amongst the Purusha:s (i.e. Individual souls)

sarvas sarvas sivas stha:nuhu bhu:tha:dir nidhiravyayaha |
sambhavo: bha:vano: bhartha: prabhavah prabhur i:svaraha || 4

MEANINGS

Sarvaha   = He who is all
Sarvaha   = The Remover
Sivaha   = He who confers auspiciousness
Stha:nuhu   = He who is firm (in blessing others)
Bhu:tha:dihi   = He who is eagerly resorted to by all
Nidhir avyayaha = The inexhaustible treasure
Sambhavaha   = He who manifests Himself
Bha:vanaha   = Savior
Bhartha: = Supporter
Prabhavaha   = He of exalted birth
Prabhuhu   = He who is all powerful
I:svaraha   = The Supreme Ruler

svayambhu:s sambhur a:dithyah pushkara:ksho: maha:svanaha |
ana:di nidhano: dha:tha: vidha:tha: dha:thur uththamaha || 5

MEANINGS

Svayam - bhu:hu   = He who manifests Himself
Sambhu:hu   = The Source of happiness. He is 'Sambhu' because He
                        causes 'sam' (Happiness) to all by manifesting thus
                        His beauty, availability and other qualities
A:dithyaha   = The Person in the Sun
Pushkara:kshaha   = The Lotus eyed
Maha:-svanaha   = He of venerable sound
Ana:di nidhanaha   = One who is without beginning or end
Dha:tha: = The creator
Vidha:tha: = The Producer
Dha:thur uththamaha = Far Superior to Bramha

aprame:yo: hrushi:ke:sah padmana:bho: amaraprabhuhu |
visvakarma: manus thvashta: sthavishtas sthaviro: dhruvaha || 6

MEANINGS

Aprame:yaha   = The immeasurable
Hrushi:ke:saha   = The controller of the sense - organs
Padmana:bhaha   = He who has a lotus in the navel
Amara Prabhuhu   = The powerful Lord of the immortal gods
Visva Karma: = He who is the agent of all actions (in regard to the
                     universe)
Manuhu   = He who wills
Thwashta: = The chiseler
Sthavishtaha   = He who is exceedingly huge in size
Sthaviraha   = He who is existent at all times
Dhruvaha   = He who is firm and unchanging

agra:hyas sa:svathah krushno: lo:hitha:kshah prathardanaha |
prabhu:thas thrikakubdha:ma pavithram mangalam param || 7

MEANINGS

Agra:hyaha	=	One who is beyond the grasp (of others)
Sa:svathaha	=	The Eternal
Krushnaha	=	He who is exceedingly delighted
Lo:hitha:kshaha	=	The Red -eyed
Prathardanaha	=	The Destroyer
Prabhu:thaha	=	He who is affluent.
Thrikakubdha:ma	=	He who has the three-fold world as His abode.
Pavithram	=	Purity Incarnate.
Mangalam Param	=	The Embodiment of Supreme Auspiciousness, which is opposed to all that is of the nature of a blemish.

I:sa:nah pra:nadah pra:no: jye:shtas sre:shtah praja:pathihi |
hiranyagarbho: bhu:garbho: ma:dhavo: madhusu:danaha || 8

MEANINGS

Isa:naha	=	The controller.
Pra:nadaha	=	The life-giver.
Pra:naha	=	Life.
Jye:shttah	=	Highly praise - worthy.
Sre:shtaha	=	The Pre-eminent
Praja:pathihi	=	Lord of the Ever-free Angels
Hiranya garbhah	=	He who is in a lovely Abode.
Bhu:garbhaha	=	He for whom Earth is the object of protection.
Ma:dhava:ha	=	The consort of Ma: (i.e. Lakshmi) Ma:ya:h - of Sri: Dhavah - The Husband; i.e. The Consort of Lakshmi.
Madhusu:danaha	=	The Slayer of Madhu.

I:svaro: vikrami: dhanvi: me:dha: vi: vikramah kramaha |
anuththamo: dura:dharshaha kruthajnah kruthir a:thmava:n || 9

MEANINGS

I:svaraha	=	The Ruler.
Vikrami:	=	The most powerful
Dhanvi:	=	The wielder of the bow.
Me:dha:vi:	=	The Omniscient
Vikramaha	=	He who moves about on the bird (Garuda)
Kramaha	=	He who is prosperous.
Anuththamaha	=	The unsurpassed. Vide -
Dura:dharshaha	=	Who is unassailable
Kruthajnaha	=	He who is grateful
Kruthihi	=	He is Himself that act
A:thmava:n	=	The possessor of the souls

sure:sas saranam sarma visvare:tha:h praja: bhavaha |
ahas samvathsaro: vya:laha prathyayas sarva darsanaha || 10

MEANINGS

Sure:saha	=	The Lord of the god
Saranam	=	The Refuge
Sarma	=	Bliss
Visvare:tha:ha	=	He whose creation, the universe is
Praja:bhavaha	=	The abode of the Praja:s (i.e. living beings)
Ahaha	=	He who never forsakes (any one)
Samvathsaraha	=	He who lives
Vya:laha	=	He who accepts (the devotees)
Prathyayaha	=	One who can be relied upon
Sarva - darsanaha	=	He who displays all (His glory)

ajas sarve: svaras siddhas siddhis sarva:dir achyuthaha |
vrusha:kapir ame:ya:thma: sarvayo:ga vinissruthaha || 11

MEANINGS

Ajaha	=	Remover (of all obstacles)
Sarve:svaraha	=	He who reaches all
Siddhaha	=	He who is ever -existing
Siddhihi	=	Goal
Sarva:dihi	=	The source of all
Achyutha:ha	=	He who is never separated
Vrusha:kapihi	=	Vara:ha, the Dharma Incarnate
Ame:ya:thma:	=	He who is of an Incomprehensible nature
Sarva yo:ga-vinissruthaha	=	He who can be attained by all means

vasur vasumana:s sathyas sama:thma: sammithas samaha |
amo:ghah pundari:ka:ksho: vrushakarma: vrusha:kruthihi || 12

MEANINGS

Vasuhu	=	He who dwells
Vasu mana:ha	=	He who has a heart which thinks of His devotees as a treasure
Sathyaha	=	He who is well-disposed
Sama:thma:	=	He whose mind is uniformly disposed
Sammithaha	=	He who has been rightly understood
Samaha	=	He who is of a uniform disposition
Amo:ghaha	=	He who is never futile
Pundari:ka:kshaha	=	The eye of Pundari:ka, i.e. the Transcendental world
Vrusha-Karma:	=	He of righteous actions
Vrusha:kruthihi	=	He of Dha:rmic form

rudro: bahusira: babhruhu visvayo:nis suchissrava:ha |
amruthas sa:svathas stha:nuhu vara:ro:ho: maha:thapa:ha ||　　　13

MEANINGS

Rudraha	=	He who makes (devotees) shed tears (of joy)
Bahu-sira:ha	=	Multi-headed
Bhabhruhu	=	The supporter
Visva-yo:nihi	=	He who associates Himself with all
Suchissrava:ha	=	He who listens to the pure words
Amruthaha	=	The Ambrosia
Sa:svathas sththa:nuhu	=	He who is eternal and steady
Vara:ro:haha	=	He who is the Supreme object of attainment
Maha: - thapa:ha	=	He who is endowed with great knowledge

sarvagas sarvavid bha:nuhu vishvakse:no: jana:rdanaha |
ve:do: ve:david avyango: ve:da:ngo: ve:davith kavihi ||　　　14

MEANINGS

Sarvagaha	=	He who reaches all
Sarva-vith	=	He who obtains all
Bha:nuhu	=	He who shines
Vishvakse:naha	=	He who is equipped with an army in all directions for the protection of all
Jana:rdhanaha	=	The destroyer of persons (who are antagonistic)
Ve:daha	=	The profounder of the Ve:da:s
Ve:davith	=	The knower of the Ve:da:s
Avyangaha	=	He who is not bereft of the limbs (of the Ve:da:s)
Ve:da:ngaha	=	He who has the Ve:da:s as His body
Ve:davith	=	He who makes people practice what is laid down in the Ve:da:s
Kavihi	=	He who sees beyond

lo:ka:dhyakshas sura:dhyaksho: dharma:dhyakshah krutha:kruthaha |
chathura:thma: chathurvyu:has chathur damshtras chathurbhujaha ||　　　15

MEANINGS

Lo:ka:dhyakshaha	=	He who controls the world
Sura:dhyakshaha	=	He who controls the gods
Dharma:dhyakshaha	=	He who controls Dharma
Krutha-akruthaha	=	The grantor of the fruits in this world and in the other
Chathura:thma:	=	He of four forms
Chathur - vyu:haha	=	He who is with four forms
Chathur-Damshtrah	=	He of four teeth
Chathur-bhujaha	=	He of four arms

bhra:jishnur bho:janam bho:ktha: sahishnur jagada:dijaha |
anagho: vijayo: je:tha: visvayo:nih punarvasuhu || 16

MEANINGS

Bhra:jishnuhu	=	The effulgent
Bho:janam	=	Food (i.e. the object of enjoyment)
Bho:ktha:	=	The Enjoyer
Sahishnuhu	=	The forgiver
Jagada:dijaha	=	He who was born at the beginning of the Universe
Anaghaha	=	Sinless
Vijayaha	=	He who was born at the beginning of the Universe
Je:thre:	=	The conqueror
Visva Yo:nihi	=	The Cause of the Universe which is Ka:rya (an effect)
Punar vasuhu	=	He who lives (in them) again and again.

upe:ndro: va:manah pra:msuhu amo:ghas suchir u:rjithaha |
athi:ndras sangrahas sargo: dhrutha:thma: niyamo: yamaha || 17

MEANINGS

Upe:ndraha	=	The brother of Indra.
Va:manaha	=	The Dwarf.
Pra:msuhu	=	The tall.
Amo:ghaha	=	He who is never purposeless.
Suchihi	=	pure.
U:rjithaha	=	He who is endowed with strength.
Athi:ndraha	=	He who excels Indra.
Sangrahaha	=	He who is easily reached.
Sargaha	=	He who creates Himself.
Dhrutha:thma:	=	The savior of the Souls.
Niyamaha	=	The controller.
Yamaha	=	The Ruler.

ve:dyo: vaidyas sada:yo:gi: vi:raha: ma:dhavo: madhuhu |
athi:ndriyo: maha:ma:yo: maho:thsa:ho: maha:balaha || 18

MEANINGS

Ve:dyaha	=	He who can be realized.
Vaidyaha	=	The knower of Vidya or knowledge.
Sada: Yogi:	=	He who is ever wide awake
Vi:raha:	=	The slayer of strong men (of wicked nature.)
Ma:dhavaha	=	The profounder of the knowledge of the Supreme Being.
Madhuhu	=	Sweet like honey.
Athi:ndriyaha	=	He who is beyond the range of the sense organs.
Maha:-ma:yaha	=	He who is possessed of Ma:ya: or wonderful power of enchantment.
Maho:thsa:haha	=	He of great enthusiasm.
Maha:-balaha	=	He of immense strength.

maha:buddhir maha:vi:ryo: maha:**s**akthir maha:dyuthihi |
anirde:**s**yavapu**s** **s**ri:ma:n ame:ya:thma: maha:dridhruth || 19

MEANINGS

Maha: - buddhihi	=	He of infinite knowledge.
Maha:-Vi:ryaha	=	He of great virility.
Maha:**s**akthihi	=	of immense power.
Maha: dyuthihi	=	He of great splendor.
Anirde:**s**ya-vapuhu	=	He who is possessed of an indescribable body.
Sri:ma:n	=	Possessed of beauty.
Ame:ya:thma:	=	He of an incomprehensible nature.
Maha:dri-dhruth	=	The bearer of the great mountain (Mandara).

mahe:shva:so: mahi:bhartha: **s**ri:niva:sas satha:m gathihi |
aniruddhas sura:nando: go:vindo: go:vida:m pathihi || 20

MEANINGS

Mahe:shwa:saha	=	The discharger of great arrows. (Literally it means the wielder of the mighty bow).
Mahi: bhartha:	=	The bearer of the earth.
Sri:niva:saha	=	In whom Lakshmi resides.
Satha:m gathihi	=	The refuge of the pious.
Aniruddhaha	=	The Irresistible.
Sura:nandaha	=	Source of delight to the gods.
Go:vindaha	=	The recipient of words (of praise)
Go:vidam Pathihi	=	The protector of those who know the words.

mari:chir damano: hamsaha supar**n**o: bhujago:ththamaha |
hira**n**yana:bhas suthapa:h padmana:bhah praja:pathihi || 21

MEANINGS

Mari:chihi	=	Ray (of light).
Damanaha	=	Dispeller.
Hamsaha	=	Swan.
Supar**n**aha	=	possessed of lovely feathers.
Bhujago:ththamaha	=	The Master of the Serpent.
Hira**n**ya na:bhaha	=	He who is possessed of a lovely navel.
Suthapa:ha	=	He who is possessed of Supreme knowledge.
Padmana:bhaha	=	He who is possessed of Lotus like navel.
Praja:-pathihi	=	The Lord of beings.

amruthyus sarvadruk simhaha sandha:tha: sandhima:n s**th**iraha |
ajo: durmarshanas **s**a:stha: vi**s**rutha:thma: sura:riha: || 22

MEANINGS

Amruthyuhu	=	The foe of Mruthyu (Death).
Sarva-druk	=	He who sees all.
Simhaha	=	The lion.
Sandha:tha:	=	He who makes His devotees join Him.
Sandhima:n	=	He who has the company.
S**th**iraha	=	He who is firm.
Ajaha	=	The Birthless.
Durmarsha**n**aha	=	The Unassailable.
Sa:stha:	=	The Chastiser.
Vi**s**rutha:thma:	=	He whose exploits are heard (with wonder).
Sura:riha:	=	The Slayer of the enemy of gods.

gurur guruthamo: dha:ma sathyas sathya para:kramaha |
nimisho: animishas sragvi: va:chaspathir udà:radhi:hi || 23

MEANINGS

Guruh Guru Thamaha	=	The foremost among the Preceptors.
Dha:ma	=	The place of Residence.
Sathyaha	=	The Good.
Sathya-Para:kramaha	=	He of truthful acts.
Nimishaha	=	He with His eyes closed.
Animishaha	=	He with His eyes closed.
Sragvi:	=	adorned with a garland.
Va:chaspathihi	=	The Lord of Speech.
Uda:ra-Dhi:hi	=	He of vast knowledge.

agrani:r gramani:s sri:ma:n nya:yo: ne:tha: sami:ranaha |
sahasra mu:rdha: visva:thma: sahasra:kshas sahasra pa:th || 24

MEANINGS

Agrani:hi	=	The Guide to a high place.
Gra:mani:hi	=	He who is the Leader of the hosts (of Angels).
Sri:ma:n	=	He who is endowed with wealth.
Nya:yaha	=	The Just.
Ne:tha:	=	He who carries out the commands (of the devotees).
Sami:ranaha	=	He whose actions are delectable.
Sahasra-mu:rdha:	=	The heads, eyes and feet mentioned in these names are to be interpreted as including all organs of knowledge and action as being implicit.
Visva:thma:	=	The All-pervading Deity.
Sahasra:kshaha	=	The Thousand-eyed.
Sahasra-pa:th	=	The Thousand-footed.

a:varthano: nivruththa:thma: samvruthas sampra mardanaha |
ahas samvarthako: vanhir anilo: dharani:dharaha || 25

MEANINGS

A:varthanaha	=	He Who turns (the wheel of Samsa:ra).
Nivruththa:thma:	=	He whose Nature rises above (other things).
Samvruthaha	=	He who remains hidden.
Sampramardanaha	=	The Dispeller.
Ahas-Samvarthakaha	=	He who turns the day.
Vanhihi	=	The Bearer.
Anilaha	=	The Giver of life-breath.
Dharani :Dharaha	=	The bearer of the Earth.

suprasa:dah prasanna:thma: visvasrud visvabhug vibhuhu |

sathkartha: sathkruthas sa:dhuhu janhur na:ra:yano: naraha || 26

MEANINGS

Suprasa:daha	=	The Conferrer of favors.
Prasanna:thma:	=	The Clear-minded.
Visvasrut	=	The Creator of the Universe.
Visvabhug - Vibhuhu	=	He who pervades all things and protects them.
Sathkartha:	=	He who honors the good.
Sathkruthaha	=	He who is worshipped.
Sa:dhuhu	=	He who carries out (what they say).
Janhuhu	=	The Concealer.
Na:ra:yanaha	=	The Support of the hosts of souls.
Naraha	=	He who is imperishable.

asankhye:yo: aprame:ya:thma: visishtas sishtakruch chuchihi |

siddha:rthas siddha sankalpaha siddhidas siddhi sa:dhanaha || 27

MEANINGS

Asankhye:yaha	=	Innumerable.
Aprame:ya:thma:	=	He of immeasurable nature.
Visishtaha	=	He Who is Superior.
Sishta kruth	=	He Who makes all persons eminent.
Suchihi	=	He Who is pure.
Siddha:rthaha	=	He Who is in possession of all desirable things.
Siddha-Sankalpaha	=	He of infallible will and determination.
Siddhidaha	=	The bestower of Siddhis or superhuman powers.
Siddhi-Sa:dhanaha	=	He Who makes the means also (as pleasant as) the goal.

vrusha:hi: vrishabho: vishnuhu vrusha parva: vrusho:daraha |

vardhano: vardha ma:nascha vivikthas sruthi sa:garaha || 28

MEANINGS

Vrusha:hi:	=	He Who has the day which is Dharma (auspicious).
Vrushabhaha	=	He Who showers (His grace).
Vishnuhu	=	The Pervader.
Vrusha-Parva:	=	He who has Dharma as steps (for His attainment).
Vrusho:dara:ha	=	He Who has a righteous belly.
Vardhanaha	=	He Who nourishes.
Vardhama:naha	=	He Who grows.
Vivikthaha	=	He Who is unique.
Sruthi-Sa:garaha	=	He Who is the sea for the Ve:da:s.

subhujo: durdharo: va:gmi: mahe:ndro: vasudo: vasuhu |

naikaru:po: bruhad ru:paha sipivishtah praka:sanaha || 29

MEANINGS

Subhujaha	=	He of lofty arms.
Durdharaha	=	The Irresistible.
Va:gmi:	=	He Who is the worthy object of words of praise.
Mahe:ndraha	=	He of great wealth.
Vasudaha	=	The Wealth-giver.
Vasuhu	=	Wealth.
Naika-Ru:paha	=	He of multifarious forms.
Bruhad-Ru:paha	=	He of an immense form.
Sipi Vishtaha	=	He Who pervades the rays.
Praka:sanaha	=	He Who snows.

o:jas the:jo: dyuthi dharah praka:sa:thma pratha:panaha |
ruddhas spashta:ksharo: manthraha chandra:msur bha:skara dyuthihi || 30

MEANINGS

O:jas the:jo: dyuthi dharaha	=	He Who is endowed with strength, vigor and brilliance.
Praka:sa:thma:	=	He of a nature that is well-known to all.
Pratha:panaha	=	He Who scorches.
Ruddhaha	=	He Who is plentiful and magnificent.
Spashta Aksharaha	=	He of clear words.
Manthraha	=	The mystic word.
Chandra-Amsuhu	=	He Who is possessed of effulgent rays like those of the Moon.
Bha:skara-Dyuthihi	=	He Who has the refulgence of the Sun.

amrutha:m su:dhbhavo: bha:nuhu sasibindus sure:svaraha |
aushadham jagathas se:thuhu sathya dharma para:kramaha || 31

MEANINGS

Amrutha:msu udbhavaha	=	The Source of the nectar-rayed moon.
Bha:nuhu	=	The Lustrous Sun.
Sasi-Binduhu	=	He Who disowns the evil-minded.
Sure:svaraha	=	The Lord of the gods.
Aushadham	=	The Medicine.
Jagathah Se:thuhu	=	The barrier of the Universe.
Sathya-Dharma-Para:kramaha	=	He Whose qualities and valor are true.

bhu:tha bhavya bhavan na:tthaha pavanah pa:vano: analaha |
ka:maha: ka:makruth ka:nthaha ka:mah ka:mapradah prabhuhu || 32

MEANINGS

Bhu:tha bhavya bhavannathaha	=	The Lord of all in the past, future and present.
Pavanaha	=	He Who moves about (Wind).
Pa:vanaha	=	The Purifier.
Analaha	=	He Who is insatiable.
Ka:maha:	=	The Destroyer of desires.
Ka:ma-kruth	=	The Creator of desirable things.
Ka:nthaha	=	He Who is charming.
Ka:maha	=	The Lovable (or Manmatha).
Ka:ma-Pradaha	=	The grantor of wishes.
Prabhuhu	=	He Who is powerful.

yuga:dikrud yuga:vartho: naikama:yo: maha:sanaha |
adrusyo: vyaktharu:pascha sahasrajid ananthajith || 33

MEANINGS

Yuga:di-Kruthu	=	The Creator at the beginning of a Yuga (aeon).
Yuga:varthah	=	He Who revolves the eons.
Naika-Ma:yaha	=	He of multifarious wonders.
Maha:sanaha	=	He Who is a voracious eater.
Adrusyaha	=	He Who cannot be seen.
Vyaktha ru:pascha	=	He who has the form that appears to His devotees.
sahasrajith	=	He who wins over through Yuga:s being in the lying posture.
Ananthajith	=	He who has the ability to remain unknown, though He is in His tiniest form.

ishto: avisishtas sishte:shtah sikhandi: nahusho: vrushaha |
kro:dhaha: kro:dha kruth kartha: visvaba:hur mahi:dharaha || 34

MEANINGS

Ishtaha	=	He Who is liked.
Avisishtaha	=	He in Whose attitude towards others, there is no difference.
Sishte:shtaha	=	He Who is dear even to eminent persons.
Sikhandi:	=	He Who has the plume (of lordship).
Nahushaha	=	He Who binds.
Vrushaha	=	He Who drenches.
Kro:dhaha:	=	He Who gave up His anger.
Krodha-kruth	=	He Who showed His anger.
Kartha:	=	He Who cuts (slays)
Visva-ba:huhu	=	He Who has arms for (the good of) the world.
Mahi:-dharaha	=	The Supporter of the world.

achyuthah prathithah pra:naha pra:nado: va:sava:nujaha |
apa:mnidhir adhishta:nam apramaththah prathishtithaha || 35

MEANINGS

Achyuthaha	=	He Who does not fall (from His status).
Prathithaha	=	He of great reputation.
Pra:naha	=	The Life-breath.
Pra:nadaha	=	The Life-giver.
Va:sava:nujaha	=	The younger brother of Va:sava (i.e. Indra).
Apa:mnidhihi	=	The sustainer of the waters of the Ocean.
Adhishta:nam	=	The Support.
Apramaththaha	=	The Vigilant.
Prathishtithaha	=	He Who is self-dependent.

skandas skandadharo: dhuryo: varado: va:yu va:hanaha |
va:sude:vo bruhad bha:nuhu a:dide:vah purandaraha || 36

MEANINGS

Skandaha	=	He Who dries up (i.e. destroys).
Skanda-dharaha	=	The Supporter of Skanda.
Dhuryaha	=	The Chief of Prop.
Varadaha	=	The Grantor of boons.
Va:yu-va:hanaha	=	He Who has Va:yu as His vehicle.
Va:sude:vaha	=	He Who pervades and sports.
Bruhad-Bha:nuha	=	He of profuse luster.
A:di-De:vaha	=	The First Deity.
Purandaraha	=	The destroyer of cities.

aso:kas tha:ranas tha:raha su:ras saurir jane:svaraha |
anuku:las satha:varthah padmi: padma nibhe:kshanaha || 37

MEANINGS

Aso:kaha	=	The dispeller of sorrows.
Tha:ranaha	=	He Who takes (others) to the other shore (a boat).
Tha:raha	=	The Savior.
Su:raha	=	The Valiant.
Saurihi	=	The son of Su:ra (Va:sude:va).
Jane:svaraha	=	The Lord of the People.
Anuku:laha	=	He Who is within bounds.
Satha:varthaha	=	He of a hundred whirlpools.
Padmi:	=	He Who has a lotus.
Padma-Nibhe:kshanaha	=	He of lotus-like glances.

padma na:bho: aravinda:kshah padma garbhas sari:rabhruth |
mahardhir ruddho: vruddha:thma: maha:ksho: garuda dhvajaha || 38

MEANINGS

Padma na:bhaha	=	He who has a lotus-like navel.
Aravinda-akshaha	=	The Lotus-eyed.
Padmagarbhaha	=	He Who is installed in a lotus.
Sari:ra-Bhruth	=	The Protector of His body (i.e. Devotees).
Mahardhihi	=	He of immense riches.
Ruddhaha	=	The Prosperous.
Vruddha:thma:	=	He of full-grown nature.
Maha:kshaha	=	He with a (vehicle of) powerful axle.
Garuda-dhvajaha	=	Garuda-bannered.

athulas sarabho: bhi:maha samayajno: havir harihi |
sarva lakshana lakshanyo: lakshmi:va:n samithinjayaha || 39

MEANINGS

Athulaha	=	The Incomparable.
Sarabhaha	=	The Destroyer.
Bhi:maha	=	The Formidable.
Samayajnaha	=	The knower of the conventions.
Havir-Harihi	=	He Who takes the offerings.
Sarva-Lakshana-Lakshanyaha	=	He Who is appropriately distinguished by all symbols which define Him (as the Supreme Deity).
Lakshmi:va:n	=	He Who is always with Lakshmi.
Samithinjayaha	=	The Victor in battles.

viksharo: ro:hitho: ma:rgo: he:thur da:mo:daras sahaha |
mahi:dharo: maha:bha:go: ve:gava:n amitha:sanaha || 40

MEANINGS

Viksharaha	=	He Who never wanes.
Ro:hithaha	=	He Who is of red complexion.
Ma:rgaha	=	He is sought after.
He:thuhu	=	The Cause.
Da:mo:daraha	=	He Who has the worlds in His belly.
Sahaha	=	He Who has patience.
Mahi:-Dharaha	=	The Supporter of the Earth.
Maha:-Bha:gaha	=	The extremely Fortunate.
Ve:gava:n	=	He Who is quick.
Amitha-A:sanaha	=	The voracious Eater.

udbhavah ksho:bhano: de:vaha sri:garbhah parame:svaraha |
karanam ka:ranam kartha: vikartha: gahano: guhaha || 41

MEANINGS

Udbhavaha	=	The Remover (of the bondage).
Ksho:bhanaha	=	The Creator of a commotion.
De:vaha	=	He Who diverts Himself.
sri: Garbhaha	=	He Who has Lakshmi always with Him.
Parame:svaraha	=	The Supreme Ruler.
Karanam	=	The Means.
Ka:ranam	=	He Who causes others to act.
Kartha:	=	The Agent.
Vikartha:	=	He Who is affected and undergoes modifications.
Gahanaha	=	He Who is deep and inscrutable.
Guhaha	=	The Savior.

vyavasa:yo: vyavastha:naha samstha:nas stha:nado: dhruvaha |
parardhih paramas spashtaha thushtah pushtas subhe:kshanaha || 42

MEANINGS

Vyavasa:yaha	=	The Pivot (of the planets.)
Vyavastha:naha	=	He who established the whole Time in Himself.
Samstha:naha	=	He who ends everything in Him.
Stha:nadaha	=	The Giver of the (Supreme) Abode.
Dhruvaha	=	The Stationary.
Pararthihi	=	He of noble and auspicious qualities.
Parama Spashtaha	=	He whose greatness is explicit.
Thushtaha	=	He Who was pleased.
Pushtaha	=	He Who is replete.
Subhe:kshanaha	=	The Auspicious-eyed.

ra:mo: vira:mo: virajo: ma:rgo: ne:yo: nayo: anayaha |
vi:ras sakthi matha:m sre:shto: dharmo: dharmavid uththamaha || 43

MEANINGS

Ra:maha	=	He Who delights.
Vira:maha	=	He before Whom all become powerless.
Virajaha	=	The Unattached.
Ne:yaha	=	He Who is governed (by His devotees).
Nayaha	=	He Who draws towards Himself all.
Anayaha	=	He Who cannot be spirited away.
Vi:raha	=	He who is the cause of terror.
Sakthimatha:m Sre:sto:	=	He who is praised by the powerful.
Dharma	=	Virtue (Incarnate).
Dharmavid-uththamaha	=	The foremost among the Dharma-conscious.

vaikuntah purushah pra:naha pra:nadah pranavah pruthuhu |
hiranya garbhas sathrughno: vya:ptho: va:yur adho:kshajaha || 44

MEANINGS

Vaikuntaha	=	Remover of obstacles (of union).
Purushaha	=	The Purifier.
Pra:naha	=	The vital air (Life-breath).
Pra:nadaha	=	The Life-giver.
Pranamah	=	He Who makes others bow before Him.
Pruthuhu	=	Well-known.
Hiranya-garbhaha	=	He, Who was in the delightful hearts.
Sathrughnaha	=	The Enemy-slayer.
Vya:pthaha	=	He Who is full (of love and affection).
Va:yuha	=	He Who moves (towards His devotees).
Adho:kshajaha	=	He Who does not get diminished.

ruthus sudarsanah ka:laha parame:shti: parigrahaha |
ugras samvathsaro: daksho: visra:mo: visva dakshinaha || 45

MEANINGS

Ruthuhu	=	He Who moves towards.
Sudarsanaha	=	He of a delightful appearance.
Ka:laha	=	He Who draws (all towards Himself).
Parame:shti:	=	He Who is in the Supreme abode.
Parigrahaha	=	He Who takes all (with Him).
Ugraha	=	The Formidable.
Samvathsaraha	=	He Who resides.
Dakshaha	=	He Who is quick in action.
Visra:maha	=	The Place or Rest.
Visva-dakshinaha	=	He Who is well-disposed towards all.

vistha:ras stha:vara stha:nuh prama:nam bi:jam avyayam |
artho: :nartho: maha:ko:so: maha:bho:go: maha:dhanaha || 46

MEANINGS

Vistha:raha	=	He Who spreads.
Stha:vara-stha:nuhu	=	He Who is tranquil after the establishment (of the Dharma).
Prama:nam	=	The Authority.
Bi:jam Avyayam	=	The Seed Imperishable.
Arthaha	=	The goal.
Anarthaha	=	He Who is not the goal.
Maha:-ko:saha	=	He Who has a great Treasure.
Maha: bho:gaha	=	He Who has objects of great enjoyment.
Maha:-dhanah	=	He of great wealth.

anirvinnas sthahvishto: bhu:hu dharma yu:po: maha: makhaha |
nakshathra ne:mir nakshathri: kshamaha ksha:mas sami:hanaha || 47

MEANINGS

Anirvinnaha	=	He Who is never despondent.
Sthavishttaha	=	He Who is of an extremely prodigious size.
Bhu:hu	=	The All-supporter.
Dharma yu:paha	=	He Who is united with Dharma.
Maha: makhaha	=	He Who is the great sacrifice.
Nakshathrane:mihi	=	He who runs the wheel of light in this Universe.
Nakshathri:	=	He Who has the stars.
Kshamaha	=	He Who is competent.
Ksha:maha	=	He Who is in a diminished form.
Sami:hanaha	=	He Who makes others work in their respective posts.

yajna ijyo: mahe:jyascha krathus sathram satha:m gathihi |
sarvadarsi: nivruththa:thma: sarvajno: jna:nam uththamam || 48

MEANINGS

Yajnaha	=	The Sacrifice.
Ijyaha	=	He Who is the object of worship.
Mahe:jyaha	=	He Who is the object of superior worship.
Krathuhu	=	Object of sacrificial acts.
Saththram	=	He Who is the Sacrifice.
Satha:m gathihi	=	The Goal of the pious.
Sarva darsi:	=	The All-seer.
Nivruththa:thma:	=	He Whose mind is turned away (from worldly desires).
Sarvajnaha	=	The Omniscient.
Jna:nam uththamam	=	The greatest knowledge.

suvrathas sumukhas su:kshmaha sugho:shas sukhadas suhruth |
mano:haro: jithakro:dho: vi:raba:hur vida:ranaha || 49

MEANINGS

Suvrathaha	=	He of good vows.
Sumukhaha	=	He with a charming face.
Su:kshmaha	=	The Subtle.
Sugho:shaha	=	He Who has the delightful voice (of the Ve:da:s in praise of Him).
Sukhadaha	=	The Bliss-giver.
Suhruth	=	The good-hearted.
Mano:haraha	=	He Who captivates the heart.
Jitha kro:dhaha	=	He Who conquered the anger.
Vi:ra-ba:huhu	=	He of mighty arms.
Vida:ranaha	=	He Who cuts.

sva:panas svavaso: vya:pi: naika:thma: naika karmakruth |
vathsaro: vathsalo: vathsi: rathna garbho: dhane:svaraha ||　　　　　50

MEANINGS

Sva:panaha	=	He Who fulls them to sleep.
Sva vasaha	=	He Who is under His own control.
Vya:pi:	=	The Pervader.
Naika:thma:	=	He with diverse forms.
Naika-karma-kruth	=	He of diverse acts.
Vathsaraha	=	He Who lives within (all beings).
Vathsalaha	=	The Affectionate.
Vathsi:	=	He Who is possessed of such loving children.
Rathna garbhaha	=	He Who is in possession of abundant wealth.
Dhane:svaraha	=	The quick giver of wealth.

dharmagub dharmakrud dharmi: sad-aksharam-asath-ksharam |
avijna:tha: sahasra:msuhu vidha:tha: krutha lakshanaha ||　　　　　51

MEANINGS

Dharma-gup	=	The Protector of Dharma (Virtue).
Dharma kruth	=	He Who practices Dharma (Virtue).
Dharmi:	=	He Who has Dharma (as an instrument).
Sath	=	He Who is commendable.
Sad aksharam	=	He Who is ever existent without decrease or destruction.
Asath	=	He who remains the same in the way one who seeks Him with untoward attitude.
Ksharam	=	The Giver of the worldly misery.
Avijna:tha:	=	The Non-cognizant.
Sahasra amsuhu	=	He Who has a thousand rays (of knowledge).
Vidha:tha:	=	The Controller.
Krutha lakshanaha	=	He Who has prescribed the distinguishing characteristics (for the pious).

gabhasthi ne:mis sathvasthaha simho: bhu:tha mahe:svaraha |
a:dide:vo: maha:de:vo: de:ve:so: de:vabhrud guruhu ||　　　　　52

MEANINGS

Gabhasthi ne:mihi	=	He with an effulgent Discus.
Sathva sthaha	=	He is in their hearts.
Simhaha	=	He Who punishes.
Bhu:tha mahe:svaraha	=	The Supreme Lord of all beings.
A:di-de:vaha	=	He Who is the first cause and is endowed with effulgence.
Maha:-de:vaha	=	The great Player.
De:ve:saha	=	The Ruler of gods.
De:va-bhruth	=	The Supporter of the gods.
Guruhu	=	The Preceptor.

uththaro: go:pathir go:ptha: jna:na gamyah pura:thanaha |
sari:ra bhu:tha bhrud bho:ktha: kapi:ndro: bhu:ri dakshinaha || 53

MEANINGS

Uththaraha	=	The Rescuer.
Go:pathihi	=	The Master of all words.
Go:ptha:	=	The Savior.
jna:na gamyaha	=	He Who is to be realized by knowledge.
Pura:thanaha	=	The Ancient.
Sari:ra bhu:tha bhruth	=	The Bearer of the Thaththva:s (i.e.Real) as His body.
Bho:ktha:	=	The Enjoyer.
Kapi:ndraha	=	The Lord of the monkeys.
Bhu:ri-dakshinaha	=	The giver of liberal remunerations.

so:mapo: amruthapas so:maha purujith puru saththamaha |
vinayo: jayas sathya sandho: da:sa:rhas sa:thvatha:m pathihi || 54

MEANINGS

So:mapaha	=	The drinker of the So:ma (juice).
Amruthapaha	=	The drinker of Ambrosia.
So:maha	=	The Nectar.
Puru-jith	=	The Conqueror of many.
Puru saththamaha	=	He Who remains with the great.
Vinayaha	=	The One who subdues even the enemies
Jayaha	=	He Who is conquered.
Sathya-sandhaha	=	He Whose promises are true.
Da:sa:rhaha	=	He Who deserves the gifts.
Sa:thvatha:m Pathihi	=	The Lord of the Sa:thvatha:s.

ji:vo: vinayitha: sa:kshi: mukundo: :mitha vikramaha |
ambho:nidhir anantha:thma: maho:dadhi sayo::nthakaha || 55

MEANINGS

Ji:vaha	=	He Who makes (them) live.
Vinayitha:	=	He who takes care of His devotees like how a King takes care of princes.
Sa:kshi:	=	The Observer.
Mukundaha	=	The Salvation-giver.
Amitha vikramaha	=	He of boundless valor.
Ambho: nidhihi	=	He Who has placed Himself under the waters.
Anantha:thma:	=	The Inner Soul of Anantha.
Maho:dadhi sayaha	=	He Who is reclining in the vast ocean.
Anthakaha	=	He Who brings about the end (of all).

ajo: maha:rhas sva:bha:vyo: jitha:mithrah pramo:danaha |
a:nando: nandano: nandaha sathya dharma: thrivikramaha || 56

MEANINGS

Ajaha	=	He Who is signified by the letter 'A'.
Maha:rhaha	=	He Who is worthy of worship.
Sva:bha:vyaha	=	He Who is to be meditated upon by those who belong to Him.
Jitha:mithraha	=	The Conqueror of the foes.
Pramo:danaha	=	He Who delights.
A:nandaha	=	He Who is Bliss.
Nandanaha	=	He who makes others enjoy extreme happiness with a least portion of His happiness.
Nandaha	=	He Who is replete (with things blissful).
Sathya Dharma:	=	He is true in His acts.
Thrivikramaha	=	He Who traverses or pervades all the three Ve:da:s.

maharshih kapila:cha:ryaha kruthajno: me:dini:pathihi |
thripadas thridasa:dhyakshaha maha:srungah krutha:ntha kruth || 57

MEANINGS

Maharshihi	=	The great Seer.
Kapila:cha:ryaha	=	He Who is 'Kapila' (of brown complexion and also an A:cha:rya (Teacher).
Kruthajnaha	=	He Who remembers the good deed done.
Me:dini: pathihi	=	The Lord of the Earth.
Thri padaha	=	The profounder of the three (Thaththva:s).
Thrida:sa adhyakshaha	=	The Savior of the gods.
Maha:-srungaha	=	The Big-tusked (Vara:ha).
Krutha:ntha kruth	=	He who slew (him who was like) Yama.

maha:vara:ho: go:vindaha sushe:nah kanaka:ngadi: |
guhyo: gabhi:ro: gahano: gupthas chakra gada: dharaha || 58

MEANINGS

Maha: Vara:haha	=	The Great Boar.
Go:vindaha	=	He Who rescued the Earth.
Sushe:naha	=	He who is equipped with an efficient army-like body.
Kanaka:ngadi:	=	He who is adorned by armlets of gold.
Guhyaha	=	He who is concealed.
Gabhi:raha	=	He who is deep or mysterious.
Gahanaha	=	The Unfathomable.
Gupthaha	=	He who is hidden.
Chakra gada: dharaha	=	The bearer of the Discus and the Mace.

ve:dha:s sva:ngo::jithah krushno: drudhas sankarshano::chyuthaha |
varuno: va:runo: vrukshah pushkara:kṣho: maha: mana:ha || 59

MEANINGS

Ve:dha:ha	=	The Providence.
Sva:ngaha	=	He who has the marks (of sovereignty) which are His own.
Ajithaha	=	He Who has the city Ajitha: (Unconquered) by name.
Krushnaha	=	The Dark-hued.
Drudhaha	=	He Who is in a gross form.
Sankarshanaha	=	He Who draws others near Him.
Achyuthaha	=	He Who does not slip down.
Varunaha	=	He Who envelops.
Va:runaha	=	He Who is with His seekers.
Vrukshaha	=	He Who is the Resort.
Pushkara:kshaha	=	He Who has nourishing eyes.
Maha:-manaha	=	The Broad-minded.

bhagava:n bhagaha: nandi: vanama:li: hala:yudhaha |
a:dithyo: jyothir a:dithyaha sahishnur gathi saththamaha || 60

MEANINGS

Bhagava:n	=	He Who is worthy of worship.
Bhagaha:	=	He Who is possessed of auspicious qualities.
Nandi:	=	He Who has Nanda as His father.
Vana-ma:li:	=	He Who has the Vana-ma:la: (garland).
Hala:yudhaha	=	The Plough-armed.
A:dithyaha	=	The Son of Adithi, (De:vaki) or He Who has to be realized by means of 'A:'.
Jyo:thir A:dithyaha	=	The Resplendent A:dithya (Sun.)
Sahishnuhu	=	He Who has patience.
Gathi Saththamaha	=	The best instructor in the path of Dharma.

sudhanva: khanda parasuhu da:runo: dravina pradaha |
divispruk sarvadrug vya:so: va:chaspathir ayo:nijaha || 61

MEANINGS

Su dhanva:	=	He Who has a splendid bow.
Khanda-parasuhu	=	He with the broken axe.
Da:runaha	=	The Splitter.
Dravina-pradaha	=	The Wealth-giver.
Divi spruk	=	He Who touches the Lord in the Paramapada.
Sarva druk	=	The All-seer.
Vya:saha	=	The Arranger.
Va:chas pathihi	=	The Master of words.
Ayo:nijaha	=	He Who was not born out of the womb (of a woman).

thrisa:ma: sa:magas sa:ma nirva:nam bhe:shajam bhishak |
sannya:sakruch **ch**ama**s s**a:ntho: nish**t**a: **s**a:nthih para:ya**n**aha || 62

MEANINGS

Thrisa:ma:	=	He Who is propounded by the three fold Sa:ma Ve:da.
Sa:magaha	=	The Sa:ma-singer.
Sa:ma	=	The Dispeller.
Nirva:**n**am	=	The Bliss.
Bhe:shajam	=	The Remedy.
Bhishak	=	The Physician.
Sannya:sa kruth	=	He Who cuts asunder (the bonds) when desires are renounced.
Samaha	=	He Who instructs.
Sa:nthaha	=	He Whose mind is always tranquil.
Nish**t**a:	=	The object of concentration has Him and His body as the object of their meditation-body, which is pure and fascinating.
Sa:nthihi	=	Peace.
Pa:ra:ya**n**am	=	The Ultimate Means.

subha:ngas sa:nthidas srashta: kumudah kuvale:**s**ayaha |
go:hitho: go:pathir go:ptha: vrushabha:ksho: vrusha priyaha || 63

MEANINGS

Subha:ngaha	=	He Who is with the eight accessories (of yo:ga)
Sa:nthi daha	=	The One who bestows the eternal peace
Srashta:	=	The Creator.
Kumudaha	=	He Who is happy.
Kuvale:**s**ayaha	=	The Controller of the Ji:va:s who wander in this world as masters of their bodies.
Go:hithaha	=	He Who manipulates the world.
Go:pathihi	=	The Lord of the (Celestial) world.
Go:ptha:	=	The Protector.
Vrushabha:ksha:ha	=	The axle of Dharma.
Vrusha priyaha	=	The lover of both Dharmas (Pravarthaka and Nivarthaka).

anivarthi: nivruththa:thma: sankshe:ptha: kshe:makruch **ch**ivaha |
sri:vathsa vaksha:**s s**ri:va:saha **s**ri:pathi**s s**ri:matha:m varaha || 64

MEANINGS

Anivarthi:	=	He who does not turn away (those who are inclined to come back to this world)
Nivruththa:thma:	=	He who is the A:thma of those who practice Nivruththi Dharma.
Sankshe:ptha:	=	He Who limits.
Kshe:makruth	=	He who does what is good.
Sivaha	=	The Auspicious.
Sri:vathsa Vaksha:ha	=	He with the Sri:vathsa on His chest.
Sri:va:saha	=	The Abode of Lakshmi.
Sri:-pathihi	=	The Consort of Lakshmi.
Sri:matha:m varaha	=	The Foremost amongst the Opulent.

sri:das sri:sas sri:niva:saha sri:nidhis sri:vibha: vanaha |
sri:dharas sri:karas sre:yaha sri:ma:n lo:ka thraya:srayaha || 65

MEANINGS

Sri:daha	=	The Glory-giver.
Sri:saha	=	The Lord of Sri.
Sri:niva:saha	=	The contiguous support of Lakshmi.
Sri: nidhihi	=	The Abode of Sri:
Sri: vibha:vanaha	=	He who owes his greatness to Lakshmi.
Sri: dharaha	=	The Bearer of Sri:
Sri: karaha	=	He who makes Lakshmi follow Him.
Sre:ya:s Sri:ma:n	=	He who has Lakshmi, the giver of wealth to all devotees, with Him always.
Lo:ka thraya:srayaha	=	He Who is the supporter of all three worlds.

svakshas svangas satha:nando: nandir jyothir gane:svaraha |
vijitha:thma: vidhe:ya:thma: sathki:rthis chinna samsayaha || 66

MEANINGS

Svakshaha	=	The Beautiful-eyed.
Svangaha	=	The Lovely-bodied.
Satha:nandaha	=	He with a Bliss that is hundred-fold.
Nandihi	=	He Who is delighted.
Jyo:thir gane:svaraha	=	The Lord of the hosts of lustrous deities.
Vijitha:thma:	=	He Whose mind has been conquered.
Vidhe:ya:thma:	=	He Who is of a submissive nature.
Sath ki:rthihi	=	He of true renown.
Chinna samsayaha	=	The Dispeller of all doubts;

udi:rnas sarvathas chakshuhu ani:sas sa:svatha sthiraha |
bhu:sayo: bhu:shano: bhu:thihi viso:kas so:ka na:sanaha || 67

MEANINGS

Udi:rnaha	=	He Who is clearly manifest.
Sarvatha:s chakshuhu	=	He who is visible to the eyes of all.
Ani:saha	=	He Who is not the Master.
Sa:svatha sthiraha	=	He Who is eternally existent and steady.
Bhu: sayaha	=	He who lies on the ground.
Bhu:shanaha	=	He Who becomes adorned.
Bhu:thihi	=	He Who is wealth.
viso:kaha	=	He Who is without sorrow.
So:ka na:sanaha	=	The Sorrow of the people resulting from the loss of contact with Him.

archishma:n archithah kumbho: visuddha:thma: viso:dhanaha |
aniruddho::prathi rathaha pradyumno::mitha vikramaha || 68

MEANINGS

Archishma:n	=	He who has great luster.
Archithaha	=	He Who is worshipped.
Kumbhaha	=	He Who is an object of desire
Visuddha:thma:	=	He of a pure nature.
Viso:dhanaha	=	The Purifier.
Aniruddhaha	=	He who cannot be blocked by anyone.
Aprathi rathaha	=	The Matchless.
Pradyumnaha	=	The Illuminator.
Amitha vikramaha	=	He of immeasurable steps.

ka:lane:miniha: saurihi su:ras su:rajane:svaraha |
thrilo:ka:thma: thrilo:ke:saha ke:savah ke:siha: harihi || 69

MEANINGS

Ka:la ne:mi niha:	=	The destroyer of the wheel of ignorance of Time.
Saurihi	=	The Son of Su:ra (i.e. Va:sude:va).
Su:raha	=	The Valiant.
Su:ra jane:svaraha	=	The Ruler of all valiant men.
Thrilo:ka:thma:	=	He Who ever moves about in the three worlds.
Thrilo:ke:saha	=	The Ruler of the three worlds.
Ke:savaha	=	The distress-Dispeller.
Ke:siha:	=	The Slayer of Ke:si (the Asura).
Harihi	=	The Green hued.

ka:ma de:vah ka:ma pa:lah ka:mi: ka:nthah krutha:gamaha |
anirde:syavapur vishnuhu vi:ro::nantho: dhananjayaha || 70

MEANINGS

Ka:ma de:vaha	=	The Desire-grantor.
Ka:ma pa:laha	=	The protector of the gifts.
Ka:mi:	=	He who has all desirable things.
Ka:nthaha	=	He Who is charming.
Krutha:gamaha	=	The Profounder of the A:gama:s.
Anirde:sya-vapuhu	=	He of indefinable bodies.
Vishnuhu	=	The Pervader by virtue of His power.
Vi:raha	=	The Valiant.
Ananthaha	=	The Limitless.
Dhananjayaha	=	He Who surpasses wealth.

bramhanyo: bramhakrud bramha: bramha bramha vivardhanaha |
bramhavid bra:mhano: bramhi: bramhajno: bra:mhana priyaha || 71

MEANINGS

Bramhanyaha	=	He Who is beneficial to Bramhan (i.e. the sentient beings and the non-sentient objects).
Bramha kruth bramha:	=	He Who controls Bramha, the creator of big things.
Bramha:	=	The Supreme Bramhan, Parama:thma
Bramha-vivardhanaha	=	He who makes the Dharma grow.
Bramha vith	=	The Knower of the Ve:da:s.
Bra:mhanaha	=	The Instructor of the Ve:da:s.
Bramhi:	=	He who has Bramha as His possession,
Bramha-jnaha	=	The knower of the Ve:da:s.
Bra:mhana priyaha	=	He Who has the Brahmins as His beloved.

maha:kramo: maha:karma: maha:the:ja: maho:ragaha |
maha:krathur maha:yajva: maha:yajno: maha:havihi || ·   72

MEANINGS

Maha: kramo: = He who provides steps for the elevation of others.
Maha: Karma: = He of great actions.
Maha: theja:ha   = He of great Resplendence.
Maho:ragaha   = He who is great and enters into the heart.
Maha: krathuhu   = The great God Who has the easiest means of worship.
Maha: yajva: = He with worshippers of a superior nature.
Maha: yajnaha   = He Whose worship is the greatest.
Maha: havihi   = He who is worshipped with supreme oblations.

sthavyas sthavapriyas stho:thram sthuthas stho:tha: ranapriyaha |
pu:rnah pu:rayitha: punyah punyaki:rthir ana:mayaha || 73

MEANINGS

Sthavyaha   = He Who is worthy of praise.
Sthava priyaha = He Who relishes the praise.
Stho:thram   = The Eulogy incarnate.
Sthuthaha   = He Who is praised.
Stho:tha: = He Who praises those who extol Him.
Rana priyaha   = The lover of the Fight.
Pu:rnaha   = He Who is full.
Pu:rayitha: = The Fulfiller (of the desires of others).
Punyaha   = The Purifier.
Punya ki:rthihi = He, the singing of whose glory also is purifying.
Ana:mayaha   = The One who bestows Good Health.

mano:javas thi:rthakaro: vasure:tha: vasu pradaha |
vasuprado: va:sude:vo: vasur vasumana: havihi || 74

MEANINGS

Mano: javaha   = He Who is swift as thought.
Thi:rtha karaha = The source for the holiness.
Vasu re:tha:ha   = The Source of luster.
Vasu priyaha   = The Treasure-giver.
Vasu pradaha   = The Dignity-giver.
Va:sude:vaha   = The Son of Va:sude:va.
Vasuhu   = The Dweller.
Vasu mana:ha   = He Whose mind is with Vasude:va.
Havihi   = He Who was handed over.

sadgathis sathkruthis saththa: sadbhu:this sathpara:yanaha |
su:rase:no: yadusre:shtaha sanniva:sas suya:munaha || 75

MEANINGS

Sadgathihi   = The Protector of the good.
Sath kruthihi   = He of lovable acts.
Saththa: = Existence Incarnate.
Sad bhu:thihi   = The wealth for the good.
Sath para:yanam = The Support for the good.
Su:ra se:naha   = He with a valiant army.
Yadu sre:shta:ha = The pre-eminent amongst the Ya:dava:s.
Sanniva:saha   = The Abode of the saintly.
Suya:munaha   = He with the delightful sport in the Yamuna river.

bhu:tha:va:so: va:sudevaha sarva:sunilayo: :nalaha |
darpaha: darpado: druptho: durdharo::**th**a::para:jithaha || 76

MEANINGS

Bhu:tha:va:saha	=	He Who is the abode of all creatures.
Va:sude:vaha	=	The Deity that presides over the twelve-lettered (Va:sude:va) Manthra.
Sarva:su nilayaha	=	The Abode of all Souls.
Analaha	=	He Who is insatiable. The Insatiate.
Darpaha:	=	The Pride-destroyer.
Darpadaha	=	The Pride-giver.
Adrupthaha	=	He Who is not proud.
Durdharaha	=	The Uncontrollable.
Apara:jithaha	=	The Invincible.

visva mu:rthir maha: mu:rthihi di:ptha mu:rthir amu:rthima:n |
ane:ka mu:rthir avyakthaha **s**atha mu:rthi**s s**atha:nanaha || 77

MEANINGS

Visva mu:rthihi	=	He who has the Universe as His body.
Maha mu:rthihi	=	He of immense form.
Di:ptha-mu:rthihi	=	He with a shining form.
Amu:rthima:n	=	He Who is the Master of even subtle things.
Ane:ka-mu:rthihi	=	He of many forms.
Avyakthaha	=	He Who is not manifest.
Satha mu:rthihi	=	He with a hundred forms.
Satha:nanaha	=	The Hundred-faced.

e:ko: naikas sa vah kah kim yath thath padam anuththamam |
lo:ka bandhur lo:kana:tho: ma:dhavo: bhaktha vathsalaha || 78

MEANINGS

E:kaha	=	The Unique.
Naikaha	=	He Who is not one only.
Saha	=	The Generator.
Vaha	=	The Dweller.
Kaha	=	He Who shines.
Kim	=	What?
Yath	=	He Who takes efforts.
Thath	=	He Who increases
padam anuththamam	=	The Supreme Goal.
Lo:ka-bandhuhu	=	The Relative of the World,
Lo:ka na:thaha	=	The Protector of the world.
Ma:dhavaha	=	The Consort of Lakshmi.
Bhaktha vathsalaha	=	Affectionate towards the devotees.

suvarnavarno: he:ma:ngo: vara:ngas chandana:ngadi: |
vi:raha: vishamas su:nyo: ghrutha:si:r achalas chalaha || 79

MEANINGS

Suvarna varnaha	=	The Golden-hued.
He:ma:ngaha	=	He of golden limbs.
Vara:ngaha	=	He of a magnificent body.
Chandana:ngadi:	=	He who is adorned with delightful armlets.
Vi:raha:	=	The slayer of the strong (demons).
Vishamaha	=	He of conflicting acts.
Su:nyaha	=	He who was devoid of defects.
Ghrutha:si:hi	=	He Who is desirous of making the world prosperous.
Achalaha	=	The Unshakable.
Chalaha	=	He Who swerves.

ama:ni: ma:nado: ma:nyo: lo:ka sva:mi: thrilo:ka dhruth |
sume:dha: me:dhajo: dhanyaha sathya me:dha: dhara:dharaha || 80

MEANINGS

Ama:ni:	=	He Who is not proud.
Ma:nadaha	=	He Who respects (others).
Ma:nyaha	=	The object of integrity and honor.
Lo:ka sva:mi:	=	The Master of the Universe.
Thri lo:ka dhruth	=	He Who supports the three worlds.
Su me:dha:ha	=	The Well-intentioned.
Me:dhajaha	=	He Who was born as a result of a sacrifice.
Dhanyaha	=	The Blessed.
Sathya me:dha:ha	=	He of true thoughts.
Dhara: dharaha	=	He who bore the Mountain (Go:vardhana).

the:jo:vrusho: dyuthidharaha sarva-sasthra-bhrutha:m-varaha |
pragraho: nigraho: vyagro: naikasrungo: gada:grajaha || 81

MEANINGS

The:jo: vrushaha	=	He Who showers splendour.
Dyuthi dharaha	=	He Who possessed a majesty.
Sarva sasthra bhrutha:m varaha	=	The best amongst those warriors who are armed with all weapons.
Pragrahaha	=	The Controller (like the reins).
Nigrahaha	=	The One who subdues the enemies.
Vyagraha	=	He Who was very zealous (enthusiastic).
Naika srungaha	=	He Who adopted diverse tactics.
Gada:grajaha	=	The elder brother of Gada:, son of Vasudeva with wife Suna:ma.

chathur mu:rthis chathur ba:huhu chathur vyu:has chathur gathihi |

chathur a:thma: chathur bha:vaha chathur ve:da vide:kapa:th || 82

MEANINGS

Chathur mu:rthihi	=	He of Four Forms.
Chathur ba:huhu	=	The Four-armed.
Chathur vyu:haha	=	He in the form of four Emanations (Vyu:ha).
Chathur-gathihi	=	He Who is in the form of the four goals or Purusha:rttha:s.
Chathura:thma:	=	The Four-bodied.
Chathur bha:vaha	=	He Who displays four kinds of actions.
Chathur ve:da vith	=	He Who is known by those that are learned in the four Ve:da:s
E:ka pa:th	=	He Whose Incarnation is only a part.

sama:vartho: nivruththa:thma: durjayo: durathi-kramaha |

durlabho: durgamo: durgo: dura:va:so: dura:riha: || 83

MEANINGS

Sama:varthaha	=	He Who comes again and again.
Nivruttha:thma:	=	He Whose mind is turned away.
Durjayaha	=	The Invincible.
Durathikramaha	=	He Who cannot be dispensed with.
Durlabhaha	=	He Who is difficult to be attained.
Durgamaha	=	He Whom it is impossible to attain.
Durgaha	=	He Who cannot be entered into.
Dura:va:saha	=	He Whose place of residence is not easy to attain.
Dura:riha:	=	The Dispeller of the evil-minded enemies.

subha:ngo: lo:kasa:rangaha suthanthus thanthu-vardhanaha |

indra karma: maha: karma: krutha karma: krutha:gamaha || 84

MEANINGS

Subha:ngaha	=	He with a bewitching form.
Lo:ka sa:rangaha	=	He Who preached essential things in the world.
Suthanthuhu	=	He Who had a powerful net of threads.
Thanthu vardhanaha	=	He Who increases the meshes.
Indra karma:	=	He who did all this for the sake of Indra;
Maha: karma:	=	He of magnanimous actions.
Krutha karma:	=	He Who practiced acts (similar to theirs.)
Krutha: gamaha	=	The Profounder of A:gama:s (Spiritual Texts).

udbhavas sundaras sundo: rathna na:bhas sulo:chanaha |

arko: va:jasanis srungi: jayanthas sarva vijjayi: || 85

MEANINGS

Udbhavaha	=	He Who has risen above.
Sundaraha	=	He Who is handsome.
Sundaha	=	He Who softens.
Rathna na:bhaha	=	He with a gemlike navel.
Sulo:chanaha	=	He of bewitching eyes.
Arkaha	=	He Who is praised.
Va:jasanihi	=	He Who advocated eating much.
Srungi:	=	He Who has a horn.
Jayanthaha	=	The Conqueror.
Sarva vijjayi:	=	The Conqueror of those who had learnt all things.

suvarna bindur aksho:bhyaha sarva-va:gi:sva re:svaraha |
maha:hrado: maha:gartho: maha:bhu:tho: maha:nidhihi || 86

MEANINGS

Suvarna binduhu	=	He Who concealed (the truth) with words of sweet letters.
Aksho:bhyaha	=	He Who could not be confounded.
Sarva va:gi:svare:svaraha	=	The Lord of all who have a mastery over all words.
Maha: hradaha	=	The Vast Lake.
Maha: garthaha	=	The Great Pit.
Maha: bhu:thaha	=	He Who considers great men as His own.
Maha: nidhihi	=	He Who has great wealth.

kumudah kundarah kundah parjanyah pa:vano::nilaha |
amrutha:so::mrutha vapuhu sarvajnas sarvatho: mukhaha || 87

MEANINGS

Kumudaha	=	He Who is with delight on the Earth.
Kundaraha	=	He who bestows of the knowledge of the Supreme Reality.
Kundaha	=	He Who grants the successive stages of higher knowledge.
Parjanyaha	=	The rain-cloud.
Pa:vanaha	=	He Who goes.
Anilaha	=	He Who is not goaded (by any one)
Amrutha:saha	=	He Who feeds with Nectar.
Amrutha-vapuhu	=	He of a Nectar-like body.
Sarwajnaha	=	The All-knower.
Sarvatho:mukhaha	=	He for Whom there are ways of approach from all sides.

sulabhas suvrathas siddhaha sathru jicchathru tha:panaha |
nyagro:dho: dumbaro: : svatthaha cha:nu:ra:ndhra nishu:danaha || 88

MEANINGS

Sulabhaha	=	He Who can be easily attained.
Suvrathaha	=	He of good vow.
Siddhaha	=	He Who is attained.
Sathrujith sathru tha:panaha	=	He Who gives distress to His enemies by means of those who were conquered by them.
Nyagro:dho:dumbaraha	=	He Who is controlled by those who stand below bowing to Him and Who is the master of the superior Transcendental World.
Asvaththaha	=	He Who stands as the controller of the worlds through (Indra and other) gods who are transitory.
Cha:nu:ra:ndhra nishu:danaha	=	He Who slew the wrestler Cha:nu:ra by name.

sahasra:rchis sapthajihvaha sapthaidha:s saptha-va:hanaha |
amu:rthir anagho::chinthyo: bhayakruth bhaya na:sanaha || 89

MEANINGS

Sahasra-archihi	=	The Thousand-rayed.
Saptha jihvaha	=	The Seven-tongued.
Sapthaidha:ha	=	He Who shines like fire with the seven kinds of fuel.
Saptha-va:hanaha	=	He Who has seven vehicles.
Amu:rthihi	=	He Who has not the form (of others).
Anaghaha	=	The Sinless.
Achinthyaha	=	He Who surpasses all thought.
Bhaya kruth	=	He Who causes fear.
Bhaya na:sanaha	=	He Who dispels fear.

anur bruhath krusas sthu:lo: gunabhrun nirguno: maha:n |
adhruthas svadhruthas sva:sthyaha pra:gvamso: vamsa-vardhanaha || 90

MEANINGS

Anuhu	=	The Atom.
Bruhath	=	The Great.
Krusaha	=	He Who is thin.
Sthu:laha	=	He Who is immense.
Guna bhruth	=	The supporter of all that are subject to him.
Nirgunaha	=	He Who is bereft of the qualities (of others).
Maha:n	=	The Great.
Adhruthaha	=	The Uncontrolled.
Svadhruthaha	=	he Whose sovereignty is innate.
Sva:sthyaha	=	he Who has a glorious status.
Pra:g vamsaha	=	He Who is the cause of the eternally free souls.
Vamsa vardhanaha	=	He Who keeps His progeny growing.

bha:ra bhruth kathitho: yo:gi: yo:gi:sas sarva ka:madaha |
a:sramas sramanah ksha:maha suparno: va:yu va:hanaha || 91

MEANINGS

Bha:ra bhruth	=	He Who shoulders the burden.
Kathithaha	=	He Who has been revealed as such.
Yo:gi:	=	He Who is endowed with super-human powers.
Yo:gi:saha	=	He Who is the foremost Lord of all Yo:gis.
Sarva ka:madaha	=	He who bestows all desires.
A:sramaha	=	He who provides an abode of rest for them.
Sramanaha	=	He Who makes them continue their Yo:ga
Ksha:maha	=	He Who helps the Yo:gi to become well-equipped.
Suparnaha	=	He Who helps (the Yo:gis) to cross (the ocean of Samsa:ra, the repeated cycle of birth and death).
Va:yu va:hanaha	=	He Who lifts up by swift wind-like Garuda.

dhanur dharo: dhanur ve:do: dando: damayitha::damaha |
apara:jithas sarvasaho: niyantha: niyamo: yamaha || 92

MEANINGS

Dhanur dharaha = The wielder of the bow.
Dhanur ve:daha = The profounder of the Science of Archery.
Dandaha   = The source of punishment (for the wicked) wicked as per
                the rules of laws and bring happiness to the world by
                following the rules of dharma as laid down by the Ve:da:s.
Damayitha: = The One subdues the enemies.
Adamaha   = He Who is not subdued (by anyone).
Apara:jithaha = The invincible.
Sarva sahaha = He Who supports all.
Niyantha: = He Who directs.
Niyamaha   = He Who ordains.
Yamaha   = The Controller.

sathvava:n sa:thvikas sathyaha sathya dharma para:yanaha |
abhipra:yah priya:rho:rhaha priyakruth pri:thi vardhanaha || 93

MEANINGS

Sathva va:n   = He Who has the quality of Saththva (under His
                         control).
Sa:thvikaha   = He that has Saththva-guna.
Sathyaha   = The Truth.
Sathya dharma para:yanah = He Who is pleased with the true Dharma.
Abhipra:yaha   = He Who is the object of choice.
Priya:rhaha   = He Who is rightly the object of love.
Arhaha   = The fitting person.
Priya kruth   = He Who does what is wanted by others.
Pri:thi vardhanaha   = He Who enhances their joy. Again, by
                         manifesting His qualities more and more, He
                         increases the joy of His devotees.

viha:yasagathir jyo:thihi suruchir huthabhug vibhuhu |
ravir vilo:chanas su:ryaha savitha: ravilo:chanaha || 94

MEANINGS

Viha:yasa gathihi   = He Who is the means for the attainment of the
                        Paramapada (the supreme world).
Jyo:thihi   = The Light.
Suruchihi   = He of lovely effulgence.
Hutha bhug vibhuhu   = He that is the light fortnight (the period in which the
                        moon waxes).
Ravihi   = He Who is praised by virtue of His being the Summer
                        solstice.
Viro:chanaha   = The Illuminant. (Year).
Su:ryaha   = The source of movement (for the wind)
Savitha: = He Who produces (i.e. the Sun).
Ravi lo:chanaha   = He Who illuminates through (the rays of) the Sun.

anantha hutha bhug bho:ktha: sukhado: naikado: :grajaha |
anirvinnas sada:marshi: lo:ka:dhishta:nam adbhuthaha || 95

MEANINGS

Anantha huthabhuk bho:ktha:	=	He Who is Indra and Bramha of immeasurable greatness.
Sukhadaha	=	The Giver of Bliss.
Naikadaha	=	He Who is the lord of those who give many things. (Literally) The Giver of not one (i.e. many).
Agrajaha	=	He Who manifests Himself before (the Muktha:s).
Anirvinnaha	=	He Who is not despondent.
Sada:marshi:	=	He Who is ever patient.
Lo:ka:dhishta:nam	=	The Support of the worlds.
Adbhuthaha	=	He Who is extremely wonderful.

sana:th sana:thana thamaha kapilah kapir avyayaha |
svasthidas svasthi kruth svasthi svasthi bhuk svasthi dakshinaha || 96

MEANINGS

Sana:th	=	The object of enjoyment.
Sana:thana-thamaha	=	The most Ancient.
Kapilaha	=	He Who is effulgent.
Kapir avyayaha	=	He Who enjoys the never decreasing Bliss.
Svasthi-daha	=	The Giver of Auspiciousness.
Svasthi-Kruth	=	The Maker of Auspiciousness.
Svasthi:	=	He Who is Auspiciousness.
Svasthi bhuk	=	The Protector of Auspiciousness.
Svasthi dakshinaha	=	He Who has Auspiciousness (to be given) as Dakshina (or fee) in the sacrifice.

araudrah kundali: chakri: vikramyu:rjitha sa:sanaha |
sabda:thigas sabda sahaha sisiras sarvari:karaha || 97

MEANINGS

Arau:draha	=	He Who is not irascible by nature.
Kundali:	=	He who is bedecked with ear-rings.
Chakri:	=	The Discus-armed.
Vikrami:	=	He Who has prowess.
U:rjitha sa:sanaha	=	He of inviolable commands.
Sabda:thigaha	=	He Who is beyond words.
Sabda sahaha	=	He Who shoulders the burden of the worlds (of cry of distress).
Sisiraha	=	He Who rushed (to render help).
Sarvari: karaha	=	He Who had the destructive weapons in His hands.

akru:rah pe:salo: daksho: dakshinaha kshamina:m varaha |

vidvaththamo: vi:thabhayaha punyas sravana ki:rthanaha || 98

MEANINGS

Akru:raha = He who was not cruel. (He who did not cut the crocodile).

Pe:salaha = He Who is charming.

Dakshaha = He Who moves quickly.

Dakshinaha = He Who is pleasing and amiable.

Kshamina:m varaha = The foremost amongst those who have endurance.

Vidvath thamaha = The best of those who know what to do.

Vi:tha bhayaha = Because of Whom the fear (of Gaje:ndra) was dispelled.

Punya sravana ki:rthanaha = He Who has made even the hearing and narrating (of the Gaje:ndra episode) meritorious.

uththa:rano: dushkruthiha: punyo: dussvapna na:sanaha |

vi:raha: rakshanas santho: ji:vanah paryavasthithaha || 99

MEANINGS

Uththa:ranaha = He Who lifted up.

Dushkruthiha: = The Slayer of the evil-doer.

Punyaha = The Purifier.

Dussvapna na:sanaha = The remover of evil dreams.

Vi:raha: = He Who removed the powerful (bonds).

Rakshanaha = The Savior.

Santhaha = He Who makes others prosper.

Ji:vanam = The Life-giver.

Paryavasthithaha = He who stands beside.

anantharu:po::nanthasri:hi jithamanyur bhaya:pahaha |

chathurasro: gabhi:ra:thma: vidiso: vya:diso: disaha || 100

MEANINGS

Anantharu:paha = He of infinite Forms.

Anantha sri:hi = He of endless wealth.

Jitha manyuhu = He Who conquered the anger.

Bhaya:pahaha = He Who may be prayed to for dispelling the fear.

Chathurasraha = He Who does what is befitting Him.

Gabhi:ra:thma: = He of deep and profound nature.

Vidisaha = He Who is far above all.

Vya:disaha = The Conferrer of posts.

Disaha = He Who commands.

ana:dir bhu:rbhuvo: lakshmi:hi suvi:ro: ruchira:ngadaha |
janano: jana janma:dihi bhi:mo: bhi:ma para:kramaha || 101

MEANINGS

Ana:dihi	=	He Who is not accepted (as Master by some).
Bhu:r bhuvaha	=	He Who is the abode of those that really live.
Lakshmi:hi	=	The Wealth.
Suvi:raha	=	He Who possesses great valor.
Ruchira:ngadaha	=	He Who bestows His lovely form.
Jananaha	=	The Creator.
Jana Janma:dihi	=	He Who is the fruit of the birth of beings.
Bhi:maha	=	He Who is frightful.
Bhi:ma Para:kramaha	=	He Who has terrific powers.

a:dha:ranilayo: dha:tha: pushpa ha:sah praja:garaha |
u:rdhvagas sathpatha:cha:rah pra:nadah pranavah panaha || 102

MEANINGS

A:dha:ra nilayaha	=	The Abode of those who are the support (of others).
Dha:tha:	=	The Preceptor of Dharma.
Pushpa ha:saha	=	He Who is like the bloom of a flower.
Praja:garaha	=	He Who is awake.
U:rdhvagaha	=	He Who rises high.
Sathpatha:cha:raha	=	He Who makes (others) go in the right path.
Pra:nadaha	=	The Life-giver.
Pranavaha	=	He Who makes them bow (before Him).
Panaha	=	He Who makes a transaction.

prama:nam pra:nanilayaha pra:nadhruth pra:naji:vanaha |
thathvam thathvavid e:ka:thma: janma mruthyu jara:thigaha || 103

MEANINGS

Prama:nam	=	The valid Authority.
pra:na nilayaha	=	He Who is the abode for all beings.
Pra:na dhruth	=	He who is the Sustainer of living beings.
Pra:naji:vanaha	=	He Who nourishes the beings.
Thaththvam	=	He Who is Essence.
Thaththva-vith	=	The knower of Truth.
E:ka:thma:	=	The one unique and Superior Soul.
Janma mruthyu jara:thigaha	=	He Who is beyond birth, death and old age.

bhu:rbhuva svastharus tha:raha savitha: prapitha:mahaha |
yajno: yajnapathir yajva: yajna:ngo: yajna va:hanaha || 104

MEANINGS

Bhu:r bhuvas svastharuhu	=	He who is the tree for the beings of the three worlds-earth, sky and heaven.
Tha:raha	=	He Who is a ferry.
Savitha:	=	He Who produces.
Prapitha:mahaha	=	The Great-grand-father.
Yajnaha	=	He who is the sacrifice.
Yajna pathihi	=	The Lord of Yajna (sacrifice).
Yajva:	=	He Who performs the sacrifice.
Yajna:ngaha	=	He who has the sacrifices of others as an accessory to what He is doing.
Yajna va:hanaha	=	He Who helps others to complete their sacrifices.

yajna bhruth yajna kruth yajni: yajna bhuk yajna sa:dhanaha |
yajna:ntha krud yajna guhyam annam anna:da e:va cha || 105

MEANINGS

Yajna bhruth	=	He Who brings about the completion of the sacrifice.
Yajna kruth	=	He Who created the sacrifice.
Yajni:	=	He for Whose sake the sacrifices are done.
Yajna-bhuk	=	The Enjoyer or the Protector of the sacrifice.
Yajna-sa:dhanaha	=	He Who is an accessory for the sacrifice.
Yajna:ntha kruth	=	He Who produces the fruit of the sacrifices.
Yajna guhyam	=	He Who is the secret of the sacrifice.
Annam	=	The object of enjoyment.
Anna:daha	=	The Enjoyer of those who enjoy Him.

a:thma yo:nis svayam ja:tho: vaikha:nas sa:ma ga:yanaha |
de:vaki: nandanas srashta: kshithi:sah pa:pana:sanaha || 106

MEANINGS

A:thma yo:nihi	=	He Who mixes others with Himself.
Svayam ja:thaha	=	He Who is self-born.
Vaikha:naha	=	He Who uproots.
Sa:ma ga:yanaha	=	He before Whom the Sa:ma Hymns are sung.
De:vaki: nandanaha	=	The Source of joy (son) of De:vaki:.
Srashta:	=	The Creator.
Kshithi:saha	=	The Lord of the Earth.
Pa:pa na:sanaha	=	The Destroyer of sins.

sankha bhrunnandaki: chakri: sa:rnga dhanva: gada:dharaha |
ratha:ngapa:nir aksho:bhyaha sarva praharana:yudhaha || (2 times)   107

sri: sarvapraharana:yudha o:m nama ithi |

MEANINGS

Sankha bhruth	=	The bearer of Sankha.
Nandaki:	=	He Who has Nandaka, the sword.
Chakri:	=	He who has the Chakra (Discus)
Sa:rnga dhanva:	=	He has the bow, named Sa:rnga which is quite befitting Him and which, by its twang and the shower of arrows issuing out of it, puts an end to the very names of His enemies.
Gada: dharaha	=	He Who bears the Mace.
Ratha:nga pa:nihi	=	He Who is armed with the Wheel in His hand.
Aksho:bhyaha	=	He Who is unshakable.
Sarva praharana:yudhaha	=	He Who has all weapons that act (against evil).

vanama:li: gadi: sa:rngi: sankhi: chakri: cha nandaki: |
sri:ma:n na:ra:yano: vishnuhu va:sude:vo::bhi rakshathu || (2 times)   108

MEANINGS

Vanama:li	=	The One who wears a garland called Vaijayanthi.
Gadi:	=	He Who bears the Mace.
Sa:rngi:	=	He has the bow, named Sa:rnga which is quite befitting Him and which, by its twang and the shower of arrows issuing out of it, puts an end to the very names of His enemies.
Sankhi:	=	He who has Sankha (conch shell).
Chakri: cha	=	He who has the Chakra (Discus)
Nandaki:	=	He Who has Nandaka, the sword.
Sri:manna:ra:yanaha	=	Lord Srimanna:ra:yana
Vishnuhu	=	He Who is all pervading
Va:sude:vaha	=	Son of Va:sude:va
Abhirakshathu	=	Protect us.

sarvam sri: krushna:rpanamasthu

O:m asmath gurubhyo: namaha

Jai Srimannarayana!

Made in the USA
Las Vegas, NV
23 February 2021